A Short Story of American Destiny
1909–2009

A Short Story of
AMERICAN DESTINY
1909–2009

KEVIN DANN

FORTUNATUS

SAN RAFAEL, CALIFORNIA

First published in the USA
by LogoSophia
© Kevin T. Dann 2008

For information, address:
LogoSophia, P.O. Box 151011
San Rafael, CA 94915
logosophia.com

Library of Congress Cataloging-in-Publication Data

Dann, Kevin T., 1956–
A short story of American destiny, 1909–2009/
Kevin Dann. — 1st ed.

p. cm.
Includes bibliographical references and index.
ISBN 978 1 59731 163 2 (pbk. : alk. paper)
1. Occultism. 2. Forecasting—Miscellanea.
3. United States—Civilization—21st century.
4. United States—Forecasting. 5. United States—Politics
and government—2001– 6. Twenty-first century—Forecasts.
7. Champlain tercentenary celebrations. 8. Hudson-Fulton
Celebration, 1909. 9. Steiner, Rudolf, 1861–1925. I. Title.
BF1999.D26 2008
133.3—dc22   2008034372

Cover design by W. David Powell
Cover image, 'Under My Thumb (History of the World Part 1)',
by Nathan Lewis, 2005, from the Collection of Andrew J. Daniels

CONTENTS

On the 4th day of July, 1609, the great Champlain discovered what I believe to be the most beautiful body of water whose ripples in response to the gentle breeze were ever kissed by the sun-light... Is it any wonder then, when we stop to contemplate this great progress and development during the last 300 years, that we should assemble here together, to help celebrate in a fitting manner that great event?... I believe that our mission is only just begun... I believe the future is to be brighter yet; I believe that the destiny of this great nation of ours is to continue on and lead in the achievements of those great things which make for the material advancement and the uplifting of the human race of the whole world.

MAYOR JOHN BURKE, Burlington, Vermont, July 8, 1909

We are not celebrating ourselves... We celebrate in [Henry] Hudson the great race of men who made the age of discovery... We celebrate the immense significance of America to all mankind. May the harmony and fraternity of this festival be an augury for the future. May the blending of races which has made possible all that we now celebrate never be made naught by the conflict of races upon the battlefield. May the spirit of this day persist, grow ever more effective in the minds of men, and this occasion be the precursor of many a festival in the years to come, marking the steady progress of all peoples of the earth who have united to make America what it is, upwards and onward, along the path that leads to perfect peace and justice and liberty.

SENATOR ELIHU ROOT, New York City, September 29, 1909

And, since around 1909, the seer is even able to indicate how, in a distinctly recognizable way, what will come has been in preparation—that since 1909, we live inwardly in a very special time.

RUDOLF STEINER, Berlin, Germany, February 6, 1917

Might it be possible today that something of infinite importance is taking place and that human beings are not taking it into their consciousness? Could it not be that something tremendously important is taking place in the world, taking place right now, of which our own contemporaries have no presentiment?

RUDOLF STEINER, Karlsrühe, Germany, January 25, 1910

PREFACE

IN THE PAST FEW YEARS OF TEACHING a college survey course in Modern Global History, I usually find myself saying at one point that "students hate history, but love anniversaries." For many if not most young people, history means memorizing meaningless and instantly forgettable dates, while anniversaries mean a memorable party with friends. Anniversaries, though, *are history*, the universal method for human beings to mark the significant moments of lived time. They act as magical magnets for meaning, drawing a whole constellation of events and characters into a relational, emotional mandala of Time.

The two anniversaries at the center of this book—the Champlain Tercentenary and Hudson-Fulton Celebration—*were* great parties, and studying them from a century away, they even become fairly interesting history. Why then, drag in the story of an obscure Austrian clairvoyant to muddle up that history? Simply put, because, while the two American 300th anniversary parties were in full swing, an anniversary of deep significance for the entire world was unfolding, and that obscure Austrian clairvoyant—Rudolf Steiner—was the only person on the entire planet who knew about it. That he even spoke about the upcoming event—the Second Coming of Christ—is still known to very few people, as that event continues to unfold.

This book suggests that for both America and the world, 1909 was marked by some extraordinary "Signs of the Times," and so shall its 100th anniversary—in 2009—be. What kind of a party we throw in 2009, I believe, will depend to a great extent upon how accurately and faithfully we look back to 1909. That I have chosen Burlington, Vermont, and Manhattan as the twin loci of my history may seem arbitrary, even perverse, beyond the coincidence that both cities celebrated 300th anniversaries of European "discovery" in that year. But if one looks at a map of the United States, and zooms in on the northeast, you will see that the Queen City on Lake Champlain, and the Great Island at the mouth of the Hudson River, are indeed linked, by a long, watery north-south line that only barely breaks in the middle, somewhere between Lake George and Saratoga, where the two watersheds diverge from one another. One might picture that geographical union and independence as an image of the historical union and independence of Europe and America. The 1909 commemorations were largely occasions to celebrate both aspects.

My narrative is predicated on a revolutionary way of conceiving of History, and of Time, and so may seem to diverge too far from acceptable norms of narrative about the past. It shares with orthodox historical narrative, however, the central premise that one can recover from the past real truths that can help us understand the present. It also shares with the Champlain and Hudson-Fulton celebrants a love of anniversaries, even if it differs dramatically from their sense of *what* we are commemorating.

A decade less a year into the twenty-first century (and a new millennium!), the year 2009 perhaps affords just enough space for some mature historical hindsight, to make sense of what the past century was all about. Though America has only, century-wise, just finished its terrible twos, the world, reckoned by the Christian calendar, has just turned twenty-one. Twenty-one has long been felt to be the age of maturity, of independence. At 21, we should be able to take whatever the world throws at us. This book suggests that though the last century brought extraordinary challenges to humanity, now that we have turned 21, there are even more extraordinary events to come.

Envisioning what is to come has always been a tricky business, and yet America has a rich prophetic tradition. When Champlain and Hudson arrived in 1609, nearly every single native nation on this Turtle Island continent had a prophetic legend anticipating the arrival of strange white-skinned men borne by floating islands. In the Valley of Mexico, for over a century before the arrival of the Spanish, Aztec emperors and their shaman-soothsayers nervously interpreted the omens leading up to the One Reed Year, certain that the completion of this 52-year cycle would bring the Feathered Serpent Quetzalcoatl's return. It is perhaps a sign of our times that though Montezuma and the Mexicans fervently believed that the prophesied return of Quetzalcoatl finally came when Hernando Cortes struck land on Good Friday in 1519, today we have psychedelic dreamers like Daniel Pinchbeck and José Arguelles proclaiming Quetzalcoatl's imminent return in 2012. Their audience is small compared with that preached to by Christian evangelicals, who see Antichrist round every liberal, universalist corner. From whatever corner of the social and religious landscape, the contemporary American prophetic tradition is a bewildering Tower of Babel.

The forked-tongues of past and present prophets have made cynics and skeptics of those of us outside the fold of the true believers. We find ourselves today a bit like Samuel de Champlain, who on many an occasion mocked the divination beliefs of the native peoples. In his journal Champlain speaks disparagingly of a shaking tent ritual conducted by his Montagnais and Huron allies, as he accompanied them on their war party in the summer of 1609 up the *Riviére des Iroquois* (the Richelieu). The shamans are contacting the spirits to give them indications about the location of the enemy, and about their own imminent success or failure against the enemy Mohawk:

> In all their encampments, they have their *Pilotois*, or *Ostemoy*, a class of persons who play the part of soothsayers, in whom these people have faith. One of these builds a cabin, surrounds it with small pieces of wood, and covers it with his robe: after it is built, he places himself inside, so as not to be seen at all, when he seizes and shakes one of the posts of his cabin, muttering some words between his teeth, by which he says he invokes the devil, who appears to him in the form of a stone, and tells him whether they will meet their enemies and kill many of them. This *Pilotois* lies prostrate on the ground, motionless, only speaking with the devil: on a sudden, he rises to his feet, talking, and tormenting himself in such a manner that, although naked, he is all of a perspiration. All the people surround the cabin, seated on their buttocks, like apes. They frequently told me that the shaking of the cabin, which I saw, proceeded from the devil, who made it move, and not the man

inside, although I could see the contrary; for, as I have stated above, it was the *Pilotois* who took one of the supports of the cabin, and made it move in this manner. They told me also that I should see fire come out from the top, which I did not see at all. These rogues counterfeit also their voice, so that it is heavy and clear, and speak in a language unknown to the other savages. And, when they represent it as broken, the savages think that the devil is speaking, and telling them what is to happen in their war, and what they must do.

But all these scapegraces, who play the soothsayer, out of a hundred words, do not speak two that are true, and impose upon these poor people. There are enough like them in the world, who take food from the mouths of the people by their impostures, as these worthies do. I often remonstrated with the people, telling them that all they did was sheer nonsense, and that they ought not to put confidence in them.

Champlain's dismissal is *our* dismissal; we assume that this performance is crude stage magic, sophomoric and deceitful sleight-of-hand. Champlain's skepticism is so complete that just a few days later, when he has a precognitive dream of a victorious battle with the Mohawks, he makes no comment about it in his journal. For a brief instant, it seemed that the European consciousness had been folded into the native one, that Champlain had himself momentarily been given the gift of prophecy. When he tells his native allies about his dream, they spring into action, mapping the coming battle in the dirt, confident of victory since Champlain has seen it in his dream. But Champlain, having stepped into the stream of Time, steps right back out, seemingly oblivious to his own role in the action.

For over a decade, I have had dreams—both waking and sleeping—that pointed to the year 2009. Odd synchronicities and small inklings accumulated, while I—like Champlain—paid them no heed. I needed maps and dreams with bigger compass than my own to discover a possible meaning for these inklings. Some of the best maps—like John's *Revelations*, the most ambitiously far-reaching prophetic map in the Western tradition—are ones that have been around for a very long time, but whose language has been forgotten. In this book you will meet modern explorers who have found the way to decipher that awesome map of world destiny, particularly as it relates—in *Revelations* Chapter 13—to America, and to these years surrounding 2009

My title—*A Short Story of American Destiny*—alludes to the subtitle of the great Russian philosopher, poet, and founder of Russian Sophiology, Vladimir Solovyov's work, *War, Progress, and the End of History: Three Conversations Including a Short Story of the Anti-Christ*. Finished on Easter Sunday, 1900, just a few months before he died, the book is a series of dialogues between five members of the Russian intelligentsia, held in the garden of a villa in the Alps. Solovyov's prefatory question sets the tone for the book: "Is *evil* only a natural *defect*, an imperfection disappearing by itself with the growth of good, or is it a real *power*, *ruling* our world by means of temptations, so that to fight it successfully assistance must be found in another sphere of being?" Along with sharing with Solovyov the same affirmative answer to that question, this book shares the conviction that America needs prophecy as much as Russia does, but true, universal, world-affirming prophecy.

*

To host an anniversary celebration, one needs to be prepared—the house needs to be put in order, invitations must be sent, vittles and grog laid in. But after everyone arrives, the anniversary only becomes a meaningful festival of memory if the guests bring their deepest powers of thinking, feeling and willing into communion with others. 2009 will be a glorious anniversary year if we enter into the commemoration prepared, with a clear and unflinching knowledge of who we are, where we have come from, and where we are going. This book is offered in that spirit of inner preparation.

—Burlington, Vermont, July 2008

I

1909: APOGEE

July 4–9: Burlington: Parades & Pageantry

THE DAY AFTER JULY 4, 1909 in Burlington, Vermont, began a week of celebration that surpassed any the city or state had ever seen. It was the three hundredth anniversary of Samuel de Champlain's "discovery" of the lake that bore his name, and both on its western shore, from Ticonderoga to Rouse's Point, New York, and its eastern shore, from Vergennes to St. Albans, Vermont, the people of the Champlain Valley were throwing a huge party. Vermont's Queen City had outdone all the other lakeside towns, planning a full week of festivities. Twenty-five thousand electric lights were installed along city streets to light the way for the more than 50,000 visitors expected. The Rutland and Central Vermont Railroads added extra cars for Tercentenary week, and the steamers *Ticonderoga* and *Chateaugay* were full on all their excursions. Burlington doubled the size of its police force, deputizing local men and hiring five Pinkerton agents from New York. City workers labored for weeks building a $9000, arc-lighted grandstand on the waterfront, and a vacant lot off South Union Street became a staging ground for the launch of a mammoth airship. On the morning of the fifth, Vermont's first marathon was held at Centennial Field; among the entries were Olympic runner Johnny Hayes; Ted Crook, who had captured the $10,000 purse just two months before at the New York Polo Grounds; and Pat Dineen, who circled the track 104 times to win the race in just over three hours. The darling of the crowd, though, was Fred Simpson, an Ojibwa Indian known to the fans by the same commemorative name as the mid-nineteenth century's most famous sports star—the Morgan trotter "Black Hawk." Each time Simpson passed the stands, the crowd let out a shrill war whoop, like the one that all of New England imagined the Sauk chief once to have yelled.

A semi-pro baseball game, a parade, a sailing regatta, a motor boat race, and fireworks followed the marathon. Visitors could also take in Colonel Francis Ferari's Trained Wild Animal Arena and Exposition out at the Allen lot on Shelburne Street, where they could see "Bertini" ascend a spiral tower fifty feet high, watch "Mamie" in her fire, snake, and electrical dances, marvel at Darling's Dogs and Ponies, "an exhibition of canine and equine intelligence," or hazard a trip through the "mile of mirrors" of the $10,000 Crystal Maze. At the Strong Theater, Bobby Daly, a cavalryman from Fort Ethan Allen, took on Willie Mango of New York City in a boxing match. At George Mylkes' Church Street magazine stand and a dozen other places around town, miniature birch bark canoes, toy bows and arrows, and French and American flags were snatched up by eager souvenir-hunters. The Hobart Shanley Company ran half-page ads in the *Burlington Free Press* for Walter Hill Crockett's just-published *History of Lake Champlain*. Burlington's streets were crowded with straw-hatted men, women in white muslin, and soldiers in full dress sweating in the July sun. The finest yachts from Canada, New England, and New York gathered around the breakwater in Burlington Bay, where there was also a torpedo boat on display.

July 7, "Patriotic and Fraternal Society Day," saw a parade of Burlington's secret and beneficial societies. A variety of veteran's organizations led the parade; the G.A.R., D.A.R., United Spanish War Veterans, and the Society of Colonial Wars in the State of Vermont. There followed five lodges of Masons, six lodges of Odd Fellows, the Fraternal Order of Eagles, Foresters of America, Modern Woodmen of America, the Royal Arcanum, and the Improved Order of Red Men. Behind them, Burlington's small army of clerks, undertakers, salesmen, wood dealers, teamsters, and laborers of all sorts filed by in full regalia, wedged between banners of the German Order of Harugan, the Ancient Order of Hibernians, the Knights of Columbus, the Knights of Pythias, and the Saint-Jean Baptiste Society. Many of these last marchers were immigrants or the children of immigrants, and one of the main hopes of the Tercentenary organizers was for the celebration's "Americanizing" influence. All week long, scores of French-Canadians, Irish, Italians, and other non-Yankees were being given a grand civics lesson by the town fathers. The fortuitous coincidence of the dates of Champlain's "discovery" and Independence Day created a perfect opportunity to encourage a transfer of allegiance by Vermont's most populous underclass, the French-Canadian, from the *fleur-de-lis* to the Stars and Stripes. While workers paraded bodies, their town-father employers paraded minds, via a procession of distinguished poets and politicians who built a narrative of the Champlain Valley's heroic past. Much of that narrative focused on the region's aboriginal inhabitants — the Abenaki and the Iroquois — and their roles in the historic drama.

In 1609, the Abenaki—the name that has come to characterize the *wābanakiak*, the "People of the Dawnland"—inhabited the region from Lake Champlain to the Atlantic. Speaking closely related but distinct dialects of the eastern Algonquian language, the eastern Abenakis—the Kennebec, Penobscot, Androscoggin and others— lived in what is now Maine, while the western Abenakis inhabited the region from Lake Champlain to the White Mountains, their northern limit the St. Lawrence River and their southern villages extending to the upper Merrimac River on the east, the Hoosic River on the west, with a number of villages along the Connecticut River in the area of what is now the Vermont-Massachusetts border. The area between Lake Champlain and the Connecticut River, the land that came to be known as Vermont, was the heart of the western Abenaki homeland.

On the other side of *bitabagw*, the "lake between" that was the center of the western Abenaki universe, dwelt the Iroquois, a people whose language, mythology, social customs, economy, and material culture were as different from the Abenaki as the Precambrian rocks of the Adirondack massif were from the Paleozoic strata of the Champlain Valley. Sometime between AD 1400 and Champlain's arrival in the region, five separate groups of Iroquoian-speaking peoples had formed the League of the *Houdénosaunee*, or Five Nations. Prominent among them, especially in the minds of the orators from Albany, were the Abenaki's western neighbors, the

Kaniengehaga, or Mohawk, who were the "Keepers of the Eastern Door" of the Five Nations confederacy. Westward lay the nations of the Oneida, the Onondaga, the Cayuga, and the Seneca.

According to one Tercentenary orator, former Secretary of War Elihu Root, the Iroquois held in subjection an area from New York to Ohio, Tennessee, and northern Virginia. Tercentenary poets recapitulated the myth in verse; Percy MacKaye's ballad *Ticonderoga* spoke of how "The Iroquois: in covert glade / They built their pine-bough palisade / And weave in trance / Their sachem dance... / Conquering the region aborigina. ..." Without exception, the speakers extolled the superiority of the Iroquois. Root, whose text began by contrasting the "lowest stage of industrial life"—i.e., hunting and gathering—practiced by the Algonquians with the agricultural and sedentary ways of the Iroquois, went so far as to say that the English would not have prevailed over the French, nor the American revolutionaries over Great Britain, were it not for the aid of the Iroquois.

The event that all this rhetoric celebrated, Samuel de Champlain's voyage up the Richelieu to *bitabagw* in 1609, was the pivotal point in the Tercentenary orators' story—prehistory's surrender to history. With Champlain's arrival, ten thousand years were compressed into a vague aboriginal mist that served only as prelude to the region's seminal event—the struggle for empire between Great Britain and France. The Iroquois-Algonquian struggle was simply a cipher for the imperial succession that followed: first, the English-French conflict, the empire of one superior European foe "naturally" succeeding its predecessor aboriginal empire; second, America's supplanting of British rule in the War for Independence; and ultimately, American entry into the twentieth century as a world power, following its triumph in the Spanish-American War.

At the Tercentenary events, the orators assigned both Iroquois and Algonquian to a vanished past. Ambassador Bryce lamented; "The monarchy of France is gone, the furs are gone, the Indians whom they sought to convert are gone." Literary critic Hamilton Mabie, whose address lasted well over an hour, finally ended with an allusion to "The Indian, survivor of a people whose story is the tragedy of the undeveloped in the path of the organized race; victim of a law which impels alike the aggressor and the exiled; oppressed that others might be free." At the Vergennes celebration the day before, Lieutenant Governor John Mead had invoked the name of "Old Long John" of Mendon as the last of the Vermont Indians. At each turn the speakers tempered their blustery rhetoric of manifest destiny with the pathos of the vanishing red man.

The Tercentenary organizers were savvy enough to realize that it was largely the educated class who listened to these addresses: to impart their patriotic message to the scores of teamsters, coal carters, and domestics who had come out looking for a little diversion from their daily drudgery, they decided to make use of a new medium, the historical pageant, which was a strange mix of costume ball, operatic spectacle, and folk play. They hired L.O. Armstrong, who had made a big splash the previous year with an Indian pageant at the Quebec Tercentenary, to produce the Lake Champlain extravaganza. Armstrong chose Canadian poet and nature writer William D. Lighthall's *Master of Life*, a play depicting the life of Hiawatha and the founding of the Iroquois Confederacy, as the historical basis for the pageant, which was enacted at each of the Tercentenary Celebration localities. The stage for the pageant was an artificial island named "Tiotiake," the Iroquois name for the island of Montreal. Six hulls (afterwards used as house boats) lashed together with cables and ten-inch square beams into three separate catamarans, were then decked over to form the "island" stage. Measuring three hundred feet by seventy feet, it included a sandy beach supported by bark underneath to keep the actors' feet from sinking. In the center a stockade of fifteen-foot tall posts surrounded an elm-bark longhouse and tepees, and at each end there were living cedar and birch trees. One tree concealed an enormous megaphone, through which the narrator of the pageant spoke. And everywhere there were lights—footlights, toplights, search lights—all illuminated by a gas generator hidden in the shrubbery. Beached alongside the ersatz island was a flotilla of canvas canoes, most of them painted to look like birchbark, while a few were authentic pine and hemlock dugouts. There was also a replica of the *Don de Dieu*, Champlain's flagship, and a group of American gunboats and fireworks boats, under the command of Commodore Armstrong.

The pageant, whose initial scenes were set sometime in the mid-sixteenth century, opened with a foot race and canoe race between the Iroquois and the Algonquins, Hurons, and their allies. There followed scenes of battle, and peacemaking by Deganawida, the "Master of Life." The pageant's dramatic action echoed the Tercentenary events, which had begun with a running race and canoe regattas, followed by the solemn peace-pipe smoking and ritual oratory of the New York and Vermont officials welcoming each other and their foreign guests. But all this was simply preamble. Following the Hiawatha portion of the Indian pageant was the event that the crowd had really come to see—the arrival of Champlain and the battle that pits him and his Algonquin warriors against the Iroquois. With a single shot from his arquebus, Champlain, played by the descendant of an early French settler, killed two of the Mohawk chiefs, reenacting the event that was popularly believed to have forged an Algonquin / Huron / Abenaki alliance with the French against the Iroquois.

Agency—the decisive, active, virile force imagined as embodied in both the Iroquois and Champlain—was the most important element communicated through the parades and pageantry. Though he made only this brief appearance in the pageant, the goateed hero could be found on nearly every street corner in Burlington. For weeks leading up to the Tercentenary celebration, merchants used Champlain's image to advertise "Special Tercentenary Sales" of hats, suits, furniture, books, furs, and even moccasins. Street vendors sold souvenir medallions of Champlain to thousands of celebrants. His noble profile exploded in the finale fireworks display out on the breakwater. Those who attended the Tercentenary speeches heard the Father of New France described in the most flowery language. Hamilton Mabie thought Champlain "the impersonation of that aggressive force of civilization which sweeps the lesser race irresistibly before it," and described him as "high-minded and generous of spirit . . . brave and hardy, of great strength, calm in danger, resourceful and swift in action." Governor Hughes of New York declared Champlain "a man of the Old World whom the children of the New World might well copy." Vermont poet Daniel Cady admired Champlain in verse: "The man who, in a tinsel age, / Cared nought for shields or bars,/Or state or showy equipage,/Whose name no scandal scars—/Whose memory, like a lofty shaft,/Stands level with the stars." French Ambassador Jusserand called his countryman "a plain, straightforward pioneer, a man of conscience, doing his duty to the best of his ability," while British ambassador Bryce placed Champlain as the last and best in an ancestral line: Columbus, Magellan, Cabot, Balboa, De Soto, Cortez, Pizarro, Cartier, and La Salle. Champlain "thought first of France and of the faith which he came to propagate, and last of himself." Father Barrett of St. Mary's Cathedral in Burlington echoed all this adulation: Champlain was "a paragon of virtue, the fearless explorer, the daring discoverer, the intrepid soldier, the untiring pioneer, the successful founder, a man among men, a born leader, a chivalrous crusader."

Many of the orators had received their images of Champlain from historian Francis Parkman, whose final estimation of Champlain—"the *preux chevalier*, the crusader, the romance-loving explorer, the curious knowledge-seeking traveler, the practical navigator"—was that he was "all for his theme and his purpose, nothing for himself." Like the orators who drew upon his histories, Parkman claimed a kinship with Champlain, prefacing his book *Pioneers of France in the New World* with a remark about how intimately he knew the locales of Champlain's exploits; he too had braved the wilderness, thrown himself selflessly into encounters with the unknown. Parkman's bluster, and that of the Tercentenary orators, revealed a deep anxiety that their own ages were less than heroic, that indeed, in a world of motorcars and urban parks, real heroism, real encounters with nature and its savages, were impossible. Living in what was widely perceived by the ruling class as an age of enfeeblement, they were obsessed with an age of heroic discovery and exploration.

There were no voices of protest raised at this devotional portrait of Champlain, no one who would have the oratory substitute "exploiter" for "explorer," "invader" for "discoverer," "genocide" for "settlement." (It would be another 15 years before William Carlos Williams, in his *In the American Grain* (1925), would spleen about Parkman's tribute to Champlain: "Good Lord, these historians! By that I understand the exact opposite of what is written: a man all for himself. . . . See if I am not right.") The 300th anniversary of Champlain's penetration of *bitabagw* was not an occasion for humility, apologetics, or restitution, or an attempt to see the event through native eyes. The reenactment of the firing of Champlain's arquebus served to fix a proper image in the crowd's mind. Percy MacKaye both expressed and nurtured the popular imagination of Champlain's mythic act in his poem "Ticonderoga." While "Maqua [Mohawk] and wild Algonquin" were taunting each other, Champlain appeared:

> And mid the silent sagamores,
> In shining cuish and casque of steel,
> Before them all
> Stands bright and tall,
> With gauntlet clenched and helmet viced,
> The calm knight errant of the Christ;
> Then, in sign miraculous,
> Levels his arquebus,
> And, charged with bullets from his bandoleer,
> Looses the bolt of preternatural thunder.

While the "mazèd" Indians watched open-mouthed, Champlain acted with the potency of his arquebus.

Other orators praised Champlain's knowledge in "Indian ways," and said that this "initiator of civilization" commanded "the almost idolatrous affection of the savage tribes of Canada." If he had given Champlain's journal of his voyage a close reading, MacKaye would have understood that Champlain was as much pawn as he was agent. On the journey south, the expectant Algonquin warriors each morning would ask Champlain what he had dreamed, hoping to gain some omen of their fortune in battle. Champlain continually dismissed their superstitious nonsense, as he did their shamans' performance of the shaking tent rite. He ridiculed the native *jongleurs,* taking their conjuring for commerce with *le Diable,* and caricatured his allies' faith in the divination ritual: "The whole tribe will be about the tent sitting on their buttocks like monkeys." But the night before they finally met the enemy, Champlain dreamed that he saw the Iroquois drowning in the lake, a favorable omen of impending victory.

For the organizers of the Tercentenary celebration, the site of the battle between Champlain and the Iroquois was a sacred place, but its sacredness was complicated by a bitter controversy over whether it was at Ticonderoga or Crown Point that Champlain had fired his arquebus. At the Crown Point celebration, Judge Albert Barnes of Chicago, who had grown up across the lake at Chimney Point, Vermont, argued that Crown Point was the authentic location, but at Ticonderoga, former New York City mayor Seth Low took a poll from the audience, who unanimously insisted it was Ticonderoga. The latter opinion won out, partly because of the hold on the sacred past that Ticonderoga possessed by virtue of its being the site of later historic events. In Percy MacKaye's poem, Ticonderoga, the "headland rock/of history," became a patriotic palimpsest, three centuries of heroism compressed into "Titans three"—the "great Chevalier" Champlain; the Marquis de Montcalm, who in 1758 successfully defended the French position at Ticonderoga against attack by the British under Lord Howe; and Ethan Allen, who led a daring "attack" on the British during the opening moments of the Revolutionary War.

MacKaye concluded his poem with a return to the mystic voice that characterized all his public poetry: "*Thine eyes grow dreamy in the evening haze,/Ticonderoga./Where, in mimic art/Ephemeral,/Thy pilgrims hold their part/In festival/On what eternal pageants dost thou gaze,/Ticonderoga?*" In this query, MacKaye was the only voice to allow the pageantry to become transparent, to acknowledge that the floating island, the mock battle, even his ballad, were all "mimic art, ephemeral." And yet he used the word "pageant" to evoke the unceasing action of history, the endless substitution of players upon the stage. For MacKaye, as for all the Tercentenary celebrants, both pageants—the eternal one and the ephemeral one—were authentic. The drama enacted at each of the Tercentenary gatherings had been staged with careful attention to creating a tangible, believable world that spectators might fully enter. *Outlook* magazine author Frank Woods wrote that the pageant Indians held the audiences "spellbound." More than 150 Indians from the reserves at Caughnawaga,

St. Francis, and Oka in Quebec, from Brantford, Garden River, and St. Regis in Ontario, and from the Onondaga Reservation in New York had been hired for the pageant. During the week of the Tercentenary Celebration, the 600-horsepower tugboat *Protector* towed the Indians and the eight white men who directed them in two boats from city to city along with the fake island. At each of the cities, for a dime per round trip, visitors could get an Indian-paddled canoe ride out to the island, where they could tour the traveling village. Scores of people posed for photos of themselves with the pageant Indians.

During the heyday of American historical pageantry, (1910–1920) there was a great attempt to involve more people than just the village elite who had traditionally been given roles to play in patriotic celebrations. Among the actors who took part in the Tercentenary pageant were schoolteachers and stenographers; veterans of the Civil War; Mohawk bridge-builders. The pageant director believed that using non-professional actors from the community would help create "mass unity" among the onlookers. There were even family ties to historic personalities among the company; one actor was descended from the Iroquois leader Joseph Brant, another, called "Scar Face" in the production, from Eunice Williams, the Deerfield captive adopted by the Abenaki at St. Francis in 1704. (The libretto claimed that "what little white blood remains in him, that little has a distinctly New England atmosphere.") The young man who played the Dutch colonial governor Corlaer was from a Dutch family who had lived at Caughnawaga for several generations. These hereditary links to the past authenticated the pageant in an almost mystical fashion, reassuring the audiences that they were experiencing faithful reproductions of the events of three hundred years ago.

A more critical element in the pageant's aim at mystical union was music. Armstrong made use of the "Indian intermezzo," which combined rumbling rhythms and minor chords to give the feeling of pentatonic harmonies backed by Indian drums. In each of the scenes when Mohawk "mystery men" or Algonquin wizards cast their spells, or when warriors gathered to raise their blood for an attack, the band below the grandstand sounded a dark, sustained E-minor chord, cueing the crowd that something aboriginal was about to ensue. The synaesthetic blend of sound and sight took the crowds in the grandstand into another world, one that was at once other-worldly and palpably *real*.

September 25– October 11: Manhattan: Aeronautics and Illuminations

On September 11, 1609, just two months after Samuel de Champlain's historic landfall, the English explorer Henry Hudson, sailing for the Dutch East India Company, anchored the *Half Moon* off the northern tip of Manhattan Island. Seeking a northwest passage to China and India, Hudson spent the next two weeks moving up the river that the Lenape people called *Mahicanituk*, the Great Tidal River. Though Giovanni Verrazano had in 1524 explored the area of New York Bay, he never came upon the great river to the north, and so, as with Champlain's 1609 voyage up the Richelieu to *bitabagw*, Hudson's 1609 expedition was looked upon universally as the advent of European exploration and discovery—and thus "history"—in the region.

From the very first meeting in 1905 of the Hudson Celebration planners, there was great enthusiasm for the idea of building a replica of Hudson's *Half Moon*. The Netherlands seized upon the idea of building the ship as a gift to the celebration. No contemporaneous portrait or model existed, but then, in the archives of the Dutch East India Company, complete plans were found of the *Half Moon*'s sister ship, the *Hope*. From these and other sources, the Director of Shipbuilding of the Netherlands Navy prepared construction plans, and the replica was built at the Royal Shipyards at Amsterdam. Century-old oak timbers from the Navy's wet dock were dried and sawn for the ship. The reproduction was faithful in every detail. There were two full decks, a poop-deck and a "tween-deck" complete with two 800-pound cannon, flanked by rammers, sponges, gunners' ladles, match-sticks, ball extractor, lanterns and pikes. The galley was outfitted with a tiled fireplace with brass-topped andirons, a pair of iron tongs and a poker. There was a set of period kitchen utensils, and a supply of peat and wood.

Hudson had a crew of only twenty men on his 1609 voyage, and the sleeping quarters had but five berths. In the forecastle the ship's creators placed three brass tablets bearing inscriptions after the manner of a seventeenth century ship: "Honor thy father and mother"; "Do not fight without a cause"; and "Good advice makes the wheels run smoothly." The replica Captain's cabin—a compartment about 5 feet 3 inches high, lighted by four windows—aimed at total fidelity, containing: one antique iron-bound treasure chest, with key; an antique medicine chest; 2 large pewter tankards; 2 large pewter plates; 5 small pewter plates; 3 large pewter mugs; 5 small dram cups (pewter); 1 pewter inkwell and sandbox, oak stand; 2 goose-quill pens; 2 pewter spoons; 1 brass astrolabe; 1 brass sundial; 1 hour glass in wooden frame; 2 single candlesticks; 2 brass candle snuffers; 1 brass hanging lamp and bracket; 1 brass firebox, with flint, steel and tinder; 2 ball padlocks; 1 pair steel dividers; 1 leather case, containing five navigating implements; 1 cross-staff; 1 mortar and pestle; 1 small earthenware jug; 1 globe; 1 leather case containing silver combination compass and sun-dial; 1 chart of the world, 1534; 1 facsimile copy on vellum of the contract between Henry Hudson and the Dutch East India Company; a book of psalms and catechism, dated 1571; a Bible dated 1568; an itinerary of Jan Van Linschoten, dated 1596; and a small sand-glass in a wooden frame.

The bow of the replica *Half Moon* was painted green, and had red and yellow ornaments in the shape of little sailors' heads. She sported an ornamental galleon and a figurehead of a red lion with golden mane. The sides of the poop deck were painted sky blue with white clouds, and the high, pear-shaped stern was beautifully carved and decorated, with the uppermost panel bearing a blue background studded with yellow stars, and a yellow crescent moon with the profile of the "Man in the Moon". Above the windows of the Captain's cabin were the coat of arms of Amsterdam with its three crosses; a red lion on a gold background —the arms of the Seven United Provinces (the seventeenth century name for the Netherlands); and the initials "V.o.C." surmounted by the initial "A"—the monogram of the Amsterdam Chamber of the Dutch East India Company.

More than Henry Hudson the Navigator, the *Half Moon* was the real star of the commemorative activities centered on Manhattan in September 1909. On the first day of the celebration, Saturday, September 25, under billowing sails and fluttering colors, the little ship (under sixty feet from stem to stern) took the lead in the largest naval assemblage in history as it moved slowly up the Hudson River. She was followed by a replica of Robert Fulton's *Clermont,* the world's first steamship. Though the hundredth anniversary of the *Clermont* came in 1907, organizers decided to combine the commemorations, given that Fulton's efforts in demonstrating the use of steam as a motive power for ships had been made on the Hudson River. Perhaps more significantly, the presence of Fulton's innovation linked the celebrants of 1909 to the primal source of their own industrial age's sense of power and progress.

For all of the attention to historical detail in the reconstruction of the *Half Moon,* or in any of the numerous educational activities inspired by remembrance of Henry Hudson and Robert Fulton's exploits, the Hudson-Fulton celebration, as surely as the Champlain Tercentenary, was not about the past but about the *present.* From the warships sent from all over the world for the fête, to the 300 dwarf cherry trees sent by Japan to be planted around Grant's Tomb and along Riverside Drive, to J. P. Morgan's exhibition of his collection of Dutch masters, to the celebrity appearances made by polar explorers Cook and Peary, this was an occasion for New York City and America to trumpet to the world its economic, military, and cultural superiority. Though set on a much humbler stage, the Champlain Tercentenary completely shared in this atmosphere of triumphalism. These historical commemorations declared unequivocally that the twentieth century would surely be the *American* century.

Champlain and Hudson had been full participants in the Age of Exploration and Discovery, but that age was not completely past. The greatest excitement in Manhattan in September of 1909 was for the possibility that an airship (it would be another decade or so before "airplane" replaced "airship" as the designation for the new vessels) might make *above* the river the same journey made by Henry Hudson in the *Half Moon* and Robert Fulton in the *Clermont.* After the Wright brothers had conquered the air at Kitty Hawk in December 1903, few dramatic advances were made in aviation until 1909. On January 1, Wilbur Wright broke the world record by staying aloft for two hours and nine minutes. (The *Times* report quoted Oliver Wright's comment that airships "would never replace railroads and ships as passenger carriers"). Louis Blériot crossed the English Channel in July. A month later, Glenn Curtiss won a speed test in France by traveling at 46.5 miles per hour over a twelve-mile course. For a week in late August, the world's premier aviators gathered in Reims, France, where Curtiss captured the $5,000 prize.

After Hudson-Fulton planners unsuccessfully courted many of the world's major aviators, Wilbur Wright and Glenn Curtiss agreed to conduct exhibition flights as part of the celebration. Wilbur Wright's contract specified $1,000 to cover expenses, regardless of whether any flights were made, with a clause promising $15,000 for a flight of ten miles or one hours' duration. Curtiss was offered $5000 for a flight from Governor's Island to Grant's Tomb and back—a distance of 29 miles. The Wright Brothers in August had initiated patent suits against the Herring-Curtiss Company, taking particular aim at Curtiss and his *Golden Flyer*, and newspaper reports of the patent suits heightened the anticipation of a Wright-Curtiss rivalry.

New York City was a very dangerous place to stage an aerial competition. Even in 1909, the city's environs presented few emergency-landing places in case of engine failure. After leaving the sandy strip on Governor's Island which had been built for the event, the aviators faced the 150-foot-tall black diabase wall of the Palisades stretching north and south along the west bank of the Hudson. On the east rose Manhattan's landscape of skyscrapers, including the brand new Singer Building, at 187 feet, the tallest building in the world. The wide, choppy Hudson River presented the only landing possibility, but it would be filled with battleships. Still, Wilbur bought a red canvas canoe from a Manhattan outfitter and hung it beneath the skids of his 1907 Model A Flyer. He also visited the Singer Building to get a sense for how the skyscrapers would influence the winds on the Hudson.

The Hudson-Fulton flights were scheduled to begin on September 27, but bad weather kept them on the ground that day and the following. Wednesday the 29th was clear, with a soft, steady wind blowing from the west. Curtiss had spent the night on the island, and shortly before dawn—witnessed only by a friend and an Army officer—he had made a flight of about 300 yards before landing again. After changing propellers, he decided to breakfast in Manhattan; shortly before 9 AM, when the ferry arrived from the Battery, off stepped Wright (who was staying at the Park Hotel on Park Avenue), who told Curtiss: "It looks pretty good. I think I will make a little spin in a few minutes."

Taking off a little after 9 AM, Wright turned two circles over the airstrip, swung east to the Buttermilk Channel, followed it to the north end of Governor's Island, then turned west and returned to the launch site. In the air for just over 7 minutes, Wright covered a distance of about two miles. At 10:18 he began a second flight, steering straight for the Statue of Liberty, a mile and a quarter to the west. The state-of-the-art ocean liner *Lusitania* was just starting out for Liverpool, and the deck was lined with passengers all waving their handkerchiefs. Wright is said to have felt the blast from the *Lusitania's* steam whistles. Tugs, steamboats—even factories—joined in the salute. Wright circled the Statue and returned at once to Governor's Island; he had been in the air less than five minutes.

This was the first flight ever made over American waters, and the only one over water anywhere in the world except Blériot's English Channel crossing and Hubert Latham's unsuccessful crossing, both in 1908. Newspapers rushed out extra editions, and the flight caused a sensation all over the city. The Hudson-Fulton Commission members were ecstatic. Before the event, one member had declared: "The climax of three centuries of progress should be marked by the navigation of the river—or part of it—by airships." Their dream had come true. Excitement built for an even longer flight, but the next four days saw bad weather, and on October 2nd, Curtiss left for another engagement in St. Louis.

On Monday the 4th the weather improved, and at 9:53 AM, Wright took off, heading straight upriver. Approaching the Battery, wind buffeted the plane, but Wright kept on. A chorus of steam whistles grew louder and louder, and crowds of people rushed to get a view of the man-bird in flight. Wright soon reached the southern end of the enormous international war fleet that stretched for ten miles north of 42nd Street. Sailors gathered on the decks and cheered. Reaching Grant's Tomb, Wright rose 20 feet to make the turn, and about 1000 feet north of the landmark, banked in a semicircle toward the New Jersey shore, passing directly over the middle of the British warship *Drake*. With the wind at his back, he made better speed on the return, covering the entire distance of nearly twenty miles in 33 minutes, 33 seconds. His average altitude was 200 feet; Wright reported afterwards that he could see over the Palisades, but was not as high as the Metropolitan Life Insurance Building tower. He said that the currents funneled by Manhattan's skyscrapers—an especially strong puff coming at 23rd Street—had repeatedly knocked him about.

Over a million people had assembled on the banks of the Hudson to watch the naval parade, and instead were treated to a historic demonstration of the world's newest transportation innovation. The flight was Wilbur's last before a public audience; an engine problem prevented him from flying again during the Hudson celebration. But thanks to these two flights, there was an explosion of interest and innovation in aviation. That interest included the militaries of the world, many of which had been gathered on the Hudson. Wilbur Wright's 1909 Hudson flights virtually guaranteed the fateful invention of aerial combat.

Those two weeks in the fall of 1909 were heady days, even for a place as used to superlatives as New York City. The *New York Times* had printed an ode to the great city on the opening day of the Celebration:

> Mighty, ay mighty Manhattan,
> Grown, while Time counted but three arrow flights,
> From bare strand and woodland and slow rising knoll—
> A handful of red men encamped on thy heights—
> To the city of millions:
> Of millions to ever the goal,
> City whose riches are billions,
> Whose might never fails,
> Whom the nations from far off salute,
> And the voice of a continent hails
> On thy festival day!

The throng perched on the Palisades undoubtedly felt this—that mighty Manhattan was the premier place on the continent, all of its past channeled inexorably into this present moment here at the opening of the century to heighten the contrast between its meager prehistory of "a handful of red men," and its destiny achieved, millions with billions, "whose might never fails." Given such a dramatic accomplishment as Wilbur Wright's conquest of the air, New Yorkers could easily feel that Hudson and his *Half Moon*, Fulton and the *Clermont,* and a whole host of intervening historical episodes were fated to unfold on *this* spot.

The skies over the Hudson-Fulton Celebration were also conquered by light—the electric era's transcendent symbol of happiness, freedom, and progress. All of New York City's competing lighting companies—Edison; United Electric Light & Power; New York & Queens; Richmond Light & Railroad—cooperated to illuminate the city's monuments, buildings and bridges. Over 100,000 lights outlined City Hall, Grant's Tomb, the Statue of Liberty, the East River Bridges, and the line of the parade march through central Manhattan. Manhattan was already the most illuminated city in America, but for two weeks it went far beyond anything ever seen on the Earth's darkened side: "Across the East River and the Manhattan Hollow Way, the great bridges appeared suspended in midair like vast festoons of sparkling gems, supported at their ends on pillars of lights. The public buildings and monuments stood out in glowing outlines like the creations of fancy rather than the substantial masses that they really were."

For Walter D'Arcy Ryan, director of General Electric's Illuminating Engineering Laboratory, such lighting effects were primitive and prosaic. At 155th Street and Riverside Drive, Ryan installed his "Scintillator"—a bank of 20 powerful searchlights furnished with colored lenses that played upon great clouds of steam generated by a 200-horsepower boiler. Twice each night during the Hudson-Fulton celebration, an hour-long spectacle—reinforced by the explosion of smoke-producing bombs—produced the illusion of an earthbound aurora borealis.

The great marvel for both planners and participants in the Celebration was the extraordinarily changed conditions since 1609. At each event, celebrants instinctively compared present with past, and were stunned by an overwhelming sense of human accomplishment and achievement. The preamble to the Hudson-Fulton Celebration Commission's final report distilled the essence of the celebration's outlook:

> Three hundred years ago, when civilization was hoary upon the banks of the Thames, the Rhine, the Seine, the Tiber, the Nile, and the Ganges, the primeval forests of the Hudson River gave shelter to no higher culture than the middle status of barbarism. Here was a virgin soil, seemingly reserved by Destiny in order that Civilization might here plant herself anew. . . . Then came Hudson's little ship and then the magic of three centuries of change. And in the harbor where Hudson saw only the hollow-log canoes of the native Indians, to-day float the treasure-laden argosies of the world; where he saw the rude bark habitations of the aborigines, now rises the second—soon to be the first—city of the world; and upon the banks of the river and in the tributary region where 300 years ago the barest necessities of precarious human existence were the measure of industry and the simplest requirements of personal adornment, the chase, and primitive warfare were the measure of art and science, now dwells a civilization which rivals that of any other part of the world.

Though the Commission admitted that there was "no more delicate, difficult, and uncertain a task for the historian than that of comparing the relative importance of human events," it declared Fulton's invention to rank supreme, not for its dramatic effect upon commerce, but for "increasing the neighborliness of nations" and "the brotherhood of mankind." In the wake of the two-week episode of historical commemoration, its organizers judged it a "jubilee of happiness":

> The Nation was at peace with the world. Civil concord blessed our people at home. Material prosperity abounded. Even man's evil propensities seemed to be suspended and the best qualities of human nature to come to the surface, for it is a literal fact that during the two weeks of the Celebration in New York City, there were fewer homicides, fewer suicides, and less crime gen-

erally than in any other equal period in the year. There were also fewer accidents and a lower general death rate than usual. There was seemingly nothing to alloy the happiness of the occasion and the people practically abandoned themselves for a fortnight to a rational festival of patriotic sentiment.

That the good people of Gotham could "abandon" themselves and still find fewer murders and suicides in their midst was no small feat, since all the optimism thinly masked a host of fears about modern urban civilization. In 1909, fully one third of New York City's population was foreign born, and the "festival of patriotic sentiment" was aimed particularly at these newcomers. "Their pride and loyalty," the Commissioners asserted, "should be as great as those of the descendants of the pioneer settlers."

The specter of steam and the rumbling roar of the locomotive hung so heavily in the air about Manhattan in 1909 that it colored the lexicon as vividly as the Scintillator lit the night sky. Musing upon the assimilative power of the Celebration, the final report reached for images of rockets and regulators:

> The power of tradition has been one of the most fundamental and conservative forces of all peoples of all times. As a body propelled through space tends to travel in a direct line unless diverted by some force other than that which drives it, so a people naturally tends to follow the impulses of the past and to adhere to tradition unless turned therefrom by other influences. Therefore the ingrained history of a nation, which in a broad sense we call tradition, serves as a balance wheel, tending to restrain sudden and spasmodic departures from the normal mode of progress. Historical culture thus materially promotes the welfare of the Commonwealth.

In this time and place of accelerated tempo, civic authorities' imagination of a "normal mode of progress" belied the deep anxieties and ambivalences engendered by the new rhythms. Manhattan had fully incarnated the dark possibilities of an all-consuming Mammon, but its leaders were intent upon its genteel governance. More powerfully than any historical tale, the celestial spectacles of aeronautics and electrical illumination—like the Celebration fireworks—dazzled the diverse men and women who looked up from below, uniting them in a magical technological communion.

Like the series of world's fairs that had inspired them—from the Centennial Exposition in Philadelphia (1876); the World's Columbian Exposition at Chicago (1893); the Pan-American Exposition in Buffalo (1901); Louisiana Purchase Exposition in St. Louis (1904)— the Champlain Valley and Hudson Valley historical celebrations were grand attempts to manifest and inculcate industrial America's Myth of Progress. At the Paris Exposition of 1900, Henry Adams had struggled mightily with this myth as he returned, day after day, to the *Palais d'Électricité* to view the 40-foot-tall electric dynamos humming their incessant industrial hymn. "Aching to absorb knowledge" from the machines, he declared himself "helpless to find it." In an essay titled "The Virgin and the Dynamo," Adams admitted his fascination for the airship and automobile engines, electric trams and whirring dynamos, but he intuited his way to a wider *Zeitgeist*, citing the "occult mechanism" of radium and x-rays. Unlike almost all of his fellow spectators, Adams felt his way past the heavyweight iron and chrome displays of horsepower to the heart of his era's "supersensual" world.

The words "occult" and "supersensual" haunted Adams's essay like Adams haunted the Exposition's Gallery of Machines, and he sensed some subterranean link between the modern worship of the dynamo and the medieval veneration of the Virgin. Still, the differences unnerved Adams: "The force of the Virgin was still felt at Lourdes, and seemed to be as potent as X-rays; but in America neither Venus nor Virgin ever had value as force;—at most as sentiment. No American had ever been truly afraid of either." Adams voiced *his* fear of the new God:

> At the rate of progress since 1800, every American who lived into the year 2000 would know how to control unlimited power. He would think in complexities unimaginable to an earlier mind. He would deal with problems altogether beyond the range of earlier society. To him the nineteenth century would stand on the same plane with the fourth—equally childlike—and he would only wonder how both of them,

knowing so little, and so weak in force, should have done so much.

Like his illustrious forebears, who had been full participants in their own revolutionary eras, Henry Adams drew instinctively upon history to restore his unsettled equilibrium. He knew that the year 1900 was not the first "to upset schoolmasters," that Copernicus, Galileo, and Columbus had all in turn "broken professorial necks." And yet there was ultimately little solace for him, as he judged his own and his peers' histories "unconscious and childlike," in their efforts to arrange sequences of cause and effect. Adams was brutally honest, admitting that where he saw sequence, "other men saw something quite different, and no one saw the same unit of measure." As learned and cosmopolitan as any American, the former president of the American Historical Association, author of what was perhaps America's first real cultural history, Adams saw faint prospect for the historian's art. The machine was the new cathedral and the new altar, and history would need to hear *its* gospels.

2

COMING IN THE CLOUDS

June—July 1909: Cassel, Germany

THE SON OF A MINISTER for the United Brethren Church, Wilbur Wright faithfully kept the Sabbath, and so none of his flights took place on a Sunday. Indeed, there was little in the way of religious ceremony during the Hudson-Fulton Celebration. The Champlain Tercentenary, on the other hand, opened with "Champlain Sunday," declared as a special occasion by Vermont Governor George H. Prouty. Reverend John Thomas—President of Middlebury College, and one of the Vermont Tercentenary Commissioners—prepared a model order of service for churches throughout the region to follow. For the pastoral prayer, Rev. Thomas offered three possibilities—a thanksgiving for peace which humbly beseeched that Almighty God, having "freed our borders from every enemy," would unite *all* the nations "in love as one family of mankind"; a prayer for the nation that asked God to protect the President, the Governor, the lawmakers and judges "from all evil"; and a prayer for Champlain Sunday, acknowledging that God had formerly led "our fathers into a wealthy place," and asking Him to "bless our land with honorable industry, sound learning, and pure manners."

There followed the Lord's Prayer; the hymn "O God, Beneath Thy Guiding Hand"; a sermon ("a patriotic discourse related to the discovery of the territory of Lake Champlain" was suggested); the singing of "America" ("My Country 'Tis of Thee"); and finally a benediction. At Burlington, 5,000 people gathered near the pageant grandstand for the service. Given Samuel Champlain's fidelity to the Catholic Church, the greatest fervor for the religious observances came from the local Catholic parishes, but Episcopalians,

Congregationalists, and Unitarians also held special services. Across the lake in Plattsburgh, Bishop Nelson of Albany began his sermon by proclaiming America's special dispensation: "The North American continent appears to have been held in reserve for the working out of a Divine purpose to which all nations of the earth have contributed and in which all are destined to share."

That same day, far from Burlington and Plattsburgh, in the German town of Cassel, a very small audience attended the eleventh in a series of fourteen lectures given by the Austrian philosopher and esoteric teacher Rudolf Steiner. Though he addressed many questions in his lecture, the key one was: "What really happened at the Baptism by John?" Indeed, the lecture series had begun on St. John's Day—June 24—the feast day of John the Baptist, and in the opening words of his first lecture, Steiner had briefly sketched the history of the June festival, finding antecedents in ancient Persia, Rome and northern Europe. In the Christian era, the marking of the period when days began to shorten and nights to lengthen was transformed into a celebration dedicated to the forerunner of Jesus Christ.

Steiner made it quite clear to his listeners that this event—the appearance on Earth of Christ—was the "turning point in time," the most important event in all of Earth history: "The Christ-event must be regarded as the most momentous of all events in the whole evolution of mankind, an event which provided an entirely new departure to the whole evolution of our earth." Steiner's answer to his own question about the Baptism focused on the occult physiology of the human being, the "subtle body" hidden from physical vision, but revealed to those like himself whose spiritual vision allowed them to see beyond the material world. In this lecture series, Steiner focused particularly on the "etheric body," the non-physical but coherent principle that gave shape—and life—to the human physical body. He reported that, at the moment of the Baptism in the River Jordan, the etheric body of Jesus—along with its two higher members, the astral body and Ego—had been lifted up into the spiritual world in order to host the descent of the Christ. All of John's baptisms were a form of spiritual initiation; by putting the baptized person in a state close to death, John allowed the baptismal candidate to journey to the spiritual world, to experience its reality, so that upon reuniting his subtle and physical bodies he had the shattering sense of himself as a *spiritual* being.

The Baptism of Jesus of Nazareth allowed the descent into a physical body of the Sun Spirit, and in Steiner's exposition, this great spiritual being had been known to each successive leading human civilization on Earth. Known as "Vishva Karman" to the ancient Indians thousands of years ago; as "Ahura Mazdao" to the ancient Persians; "Osiris" to the Egyptians, and as "Apollo" to early Greeks, this Sun Spirit had waited to come to Earth in a physical body until a time when it was absolutely necessary in order for human civilization to continue.

In these lectures, Steiner described how it was that John the Evangelist was able to faithfully report the inner and outer truth of the Baptism. Having been raised from the dead by Jesus Christ, Lazarus/John had, during his own "baptism"—his three-day journey through the spiritual worlds during the time when he was presumed to be dead—been held and supported by the Sun Spirit, Christ. But beyond this, Steiner pointed to an even more remarkable process: Jesus of Nazareth had as his own Ego the Ego of the great Persian initiate Zarathustra, and Christ was able to impart the knowledge contained in Zarathustra/Jesus's astral body into John during the three-day death sleep. The revived John essentially now held within his own memory the experience of the Baptism. Steiner identified certain Persian elements in the John Gospel, including the use in the Prologue of the word *Logos*, asserting that this expression (as the Persian *Vohumanu*) had first been used in Persian initiation rites.

Here was an astounding explanation for John's revelation; contained within this same lecture series was an equally astounding explanation for the source of Rudolf Steiner's revelation. In the second lecture of the series in Cassel, Steiner spoke at length of how he had come to know what he knew about the Baptism. Unlike his contemporary Biblical scholars, whose knowledge was limited to documentary investigation—and who thus argued incessantly over the John Gospel, whose mysterious narrative conflicted so dramatically with the other three Gospels, and with the era's intense effort to make the Sun Spirit over into "the simple man of Nazareth"—

Steiner claimed to read in a very different "book"—the "Akashic Record":

> Let us suppose the spiritual investigator lets his gaze wander back to the days of Charlemagne, or to Roman times, or to ancient Greece. Everything that happened in those times is preserved in the trace left by its spiritual prototype, and can be observed in the spiritual world. This kind of vision is called `reading the Akashic records'. A living script of this kind does indeed exist and can be seen by the spiritual eye. . . . Suppose the seer glances back, let us say, to the times of Julius Caesar. Caesar's actions, inasmuch as they were performed on the physical plane, were witnessed by his contemporaries; but every action has left its trace in the Akashic records, and when the seer looks back, it is as though a spiritual shadow or archetype of these actions were before him.

Steiner went on to say that the less such a seer knew of the "external history" of the subject of his research, the easier it would be for him to read the Akashic Record, since materialist historical thinking acted to obscure the truth of past events.

In 1909, Rudolf Steiner was not the only individual who claimed to be able to read the Akashic record. In the weeks leading up to the Hudson-Fulton Celebration, New York newspapers were filled with reports of the prophetic pronouncements of Theosophical Society President Annie Besant, who was giving a series of lectures at the Carnegie Lyceum and other Manhattan venues. "CHRIST COMING SOON, SAYS MRS. BESANT" shouted the *New York Times* headline on August 3rd. Besant and her fellow Theosophists held that Christ had earlier been incarnated as Hermes, Orpheus and Zoroaster, and that his reincarnation was imminent. Indeed, though she did not say so publicly as yet, Besant's colleague Charles W. Leadbeater had informed her that he had found the reincarnated Christ—Jiddu Krishnamurti, the 14-year-old son of a Society clerk—on the beach near the Theosophical Society headquarters in Adyar, India.

In October, 1909, Besant announced Krishnamurti as the "World Teacher," and then in 1910, Leadbeater published a series of articles that claimed to describe—from his reading of the Akashic Record—

the boy's previous lives. In Leadbeater's account, the biography of "Alcyone"—Leadbeater's name for Krishnamurti—begins in the Gobi Desert around 70,000 BC, and goes through 48 incarnations before appearing in Kannauj, India in 624 BC In his 13th incarnation, in 527 BC, in Ireland, Alcyone is the grandson of a priest named Surya, who with the help of the Tuatha-de-Danaan (the nature spirits) founded a series of sacred sites through which magnetic power would be radiated. In incarnation 19, Alcyone is a female priest possessed of great psychical powers, living in an area west of the Rocky Mountains. In his penultimate life, Alcyone meets Lord Buddha and becomes a devotee, traveling the Ganges Valley with him, and then is told that he will be the Maitreya who is yet to come.

Leadbeater and Besant's promotion of Krishnamurti as the reincarnated Jesus, in whom the Maitreya Bodhisattva (for Leadbeater identical with Christ) would incarnate, led Rudolf Steiner in January of 1910 to speak of the return of Christ, not in a physical form, but *in the etheric realm of the Earth*. In Karlsruhe, Germany, on January 25th, he spoke of how Christ went almost completely unrecognized during his own lifetime, and then posed a question to his audience: "Might it not then also be possible today that something of infinite importance is taking place and that human beings are not taking it into their consciousness? Could it not be that something tremendously important is taking place in the world, taking place right now, of which our own contemporaries have no presentiment?" Since the end of the Kali Yuga (the "Dark Age" of the Hindu human evolutionary schema) in 1899, Steiner said that humanity would increasingly gain the ability to perceive the etheric world, and thus, to have the "Damascus experience" of St. Paul, that is, to *see* Christ in the etheric realm. Like Paul, people would become "eye-witnesses" of Christ, making documentary evidence superfluous, or at least supplementary.

At the same time, Steiner warned that the materialist mind would conceive instead of an actual physical return of Christ, and that certain individuals—like Leadbeater's claim for Krishnamurti—would claim to be the reincarnated Christ. And then he pointed very particularly to the timing of the new etheric clairvoyance:

The first signs of these new soul faculties will begin to appear relatively soon now in isolated souls. They will become more clear in the middle of the fourth decade of this century, sometime between 1930 and 1940. The years 1933, 1935, and 1937 will be especially significant. Faculties that now are quite unusual for human beings will then manifest themselves as natural abilities. At this time great changes will take place, and Biblical prophecies will be fulfilled. Everything will be transformed for the souls who are sojourning on earth and also for those who are no longer within the physical body. Regardless of where they are, souls are encountering entirely new faculties. Everything is changing, but the most significant event of our time is a deep, decisive transformation in the soul faculties of man.

"If humanity overlooked these events, it would be a great misfortune," Steiner added.

Clearly, Rudolf Steiner's task for twentieth-century humanity was identical to the one performed twenty centuries earlier by John the Baptist—to serve as witness, as forerunner, and even as facilitator of the descent of the Sun Spirit into the etheric realm, just as John had stewarded Christ's descent into the body of Jesus of Nazareth. The stunning outpouring of wisdom from Rudolf Steiner beginning with his emergence as a spiritual teacher in 1900 until his death in 1925 can be seen as a revelation through which Jesus Christ spoke to mankind at the advent of His return within the etheric realm of the Earth. Even in the cascade of revelations made by Steiner in this single lecture, there was much more that he was *not* saying. His own biography was exquisitely in sync with the process of the etheric return of Christ. If one applies the analogy—identified by Rudolf Steiner in 1923—that one year in the life of an individual is equal to 100 years in the life of humanity since the birth of Christ, Rudolf Steiner's birth in 1861 came at the moment of humanity's "Moon Node." The lunar nodes are the two places where the Moon crosses the plane of the ecliptic each month. The axis of these nodes moves backward around the calendar, taking 18.61 years to complete a circuit. In the life of the individual, the return of the Moon's nodes is a herald of the spiritual awakening that will transpire at age 21, when the self is born. At the moment of the return of the Moon's nodes, each person can experience an opening to his higher self. The life work of Rudolf Steiner was to awaken humanity to the "higher self" of Christianity.

A few months before the lecture cycle in Cassel, Steiner had outlined in a series of ten lectures in Dusseldorf the nature and role of spiritual beings in the evolution of the cosmos, and indicated that the heliocentric orbit of the planet Jupiter marks the boundary of the evolutionary stage known in esoteric cosmology as "Ancient Sun." He also stated that this was the period when the human etheric body was first formed. The "body" that approached the Earth in 1909 was Christ's "resurrection body"—the physical body as it had been transformed by the events of the "Mystery of Golgotha" (Steiner's term for the events of Christ's life from the Passion through the Resurrection and Ascension). The resurrection body "remembered" that Ancient Sun period, in that it has a 12-year rhythm, like the planet Jupiter (whose exact orbital period is 11.86 years, i.e., Jupiter spends about one year in each zodiacal sign in its orbit of the Sun).

One significant aspect of humanity's awakening on the threshold of its 21st "birthday" was Steiner's teaching of astrosophy—a new, scientific, Christian astrology. A key concept of Steiner's astrology is that the human individuality *chooses* his moment (and place) of birth. For Steiner himself, this was shortly before midnight—under a nearly full Moon on the tail of the Lion, which was opposite the Sun in the middle of Aquarius—on February 25, 1861, in the tiny Austro-Hungarian village of Kraljevec. Just five days before, Jupiter made its ingress into the constellation of Leo, the region of the zodiac where dwell the beings who formed the human heart. The heart was to be the chalice, the Holy Grail in which would be born the renewed Christ impulse in the twentieth century, coincident with the return of the Etheric Christ. Rudolf Steiner's task would be to prepare this chalice.

On the exact same day as Franciska Blie Steiner's bleeding baby boy was carried off by her midwife to the St. Michael church in the neighboring village of Draskovec for an emergency baptism, the Etheric Christ began His descent through the spheres of the spiritual hierarchies: from February 25, 1861 to January 1, 1873, Christ passed through the sphere of the Kyriotetes; then the Dynamis (to November 11, 1884); the Exusiai (to September 27, 1896); the Archai (to August 4, 1908); the Archangels (to June 15, 1920); and finally the Angels (to April 25, 1932).

The Archai are the Time Spirits, and it was shortly after Christ's passage into their realm that Rudolf Steiner experienced a profound, singular, Christian initiation, which changed the entire course of his life. Up until this experience, Steiner had led a life not so different from many of his contemporaries. Having moved to Vienna in 1879 to study at the Technical University, he went on to earn a doctorate in philosophy at the University of Rostock, and then served for 12 years as an editor at the Goethe archives in Weimar. In 1897, he had moved to Berlin, where he started a literary magazine. But in 1899, Steiner published in the magazine his esoteric interpretation of Goethe's fairy tale, "The Green Snake and the Beautiful Lily," which led to an invitation to speak to German Theosophists on the subject of Friedrich Nietzsche (whom Steiner had met in 1896), and then to his work as a spiritual teacher.

1909 was truly the year that Steiner's work as a spiritual teacher quickened. On January 6, Epiphany—the day that marks the incarnation of Christ through the Baptism by John—in a room whose walls bore reproductions of paintings by Raphael, Rudolf Steiner revealed the karmic connection between the German poet Novalis, the Renaissance artist Raphael, John the Baptist, and the prophet Elijah. The year of lecturing in 1909 would conclude the day after Christmas with Steiner again speaking of Novalis, in such a way that clearly suggested that this great individuality was supersensibly present throughout the entire lecture. A couple of weeks after his Epiphany lecture, in Heidelberg, he began to further unfold the mysteries of "spiritual economy," which continued in his Cassel lecture cycle on the Gospel of John and then reached their climax in September in a series on the Gospel of St. Luke. Within these lectures in September of 1909 there began to appear a "Fifth Gospel," a suite of images of the events in Palestine that seemed possible only if they had been witnessed by Jesus himself.

According to the principle of spiritual economy, the etheric and

COMING IN THE CLOUDS   35

astral bodies of the highest human initiates do not dissolve into the spiritual world after death, but are preserved and then employed for mankind's further evolution. Raphael's many portraits of the holy family of the Luke Gospel, for example, were a result of his having received into his etheric body an impression of the etheric body of Jesus of Nazareth. In his next incarnation this same individuality would receive the Ego of Jesus. Steiner spoke of how, in the sixteenth century, it became possible for certain individuals to receive Christ's Ego, and that Christian Rosenkreutz—the first Rosicrucian—was one who experienced this. In 1909, even before he had spoken directly of the return in the etheric of Christ, Steiner affirmed that this was still possible for others as well: "For the further development of humanity, the copies of the ego of Jesus of Nazareth are waiting for us in the spiritual world. People who can strive to the heights of spiritual wisdom and love are candidates for these copies of the ego of Jesus of Nazareth; they become the Christ-bearers, true Christophori. It is their task on this Earth to be the preparers of his second coming."

"Second Coming" is not an expression that appears in the New Testament, and yet by the twentieth century it had long been in common usage. The Greek word *parousia* essentially means "appearance and subsequent presence with." In the original text of the New Testament, *parousia* is used for those prophecies which speak of a future presence of Christ in human evolution. But Rudolf Steiner knew from his own personal experience that the "coming" was already in progress, that Christ had continued to be a living presence throughout human history, though recognizable only to a few at any period. Steiner's emphasis was always upon *rhythm*, and the leitmotif that ran through all of his Christological teachings was the dynamic nature of Christ's being, and human beings' response to that presence.

Steiner's immense contribution to modern materialistic conceptions of the New Testament was his exact understanding of another Greek word—*nephele*. In his two Epistles to the Thessalonians— considered by most Biblical scholars to be the oldest part of the New Testament—St. Paul is the first to ever speak of the Etheric Christ: "Then we which are alive and remain shall be caught up together with them in the clouds, to meet the Lord in the air; and so shall we ever be with the Lord." To St. Paul, *nephele* meant "cloud," but it also meant the hazy, subtle, and wholly real realm that surrounds and permeates all living things. *Nephele* is the etheric realm; physical clouds are but one of the many manifestations of the living, weaving realm of the etheric. All of the many biblical passages that today strike our ears as meaning "clouds," speak of the etheric realm. That *nephele* now stands behind the term "nebulous" denotes the enormous change in human consciousness over the past two thousand years.

On January 12, 1910—the day that Rudolf Steiner spoke publicly for the first time of the imminent etheric return of Christ—the Sun was in conjunction with Uranus, the planet associated with the initiation of new impulses. Since August 4, 1908, as Christ moved through the Archangelic realm, a single human being on Earth had followed this journey inwardly, and was moved outwardly to proclaim a thrilling, awesome, wholly *new* cosmic narrative of past, present, and future. Only a small handful of people heard that narrative, and an even smaller number could fully comprehend it. It was just as he had hinted in his question to the audience in Karlsruhe: an event of world historical significance was transpiring, yet no one was aware of it.

The intense combination of historical retrospective and progressive prospect occasioned by the Champlain Tercentenary and the Hudson-Fulton Celebration in that very same signal year of 1909 came about because all who participated felt instinctively the propriety of marking the three *hundredth* anniversary of the "beginning of history" in the two regions. Beginning in 1876 with the centennial celebration of the signing of the Declaration of Independence, America in the late nineteenth century had marked countless hundredth anniversaries of Revolutionary era battles, and two hundredth anniversaries of the settlement and founding of towns. In 1709 and 1809, no one had taken notice of the anniversary of either Champlain's or Hudson's feats; in 1909, however, no one failed to mark his calendar both outwardly and inwardly. The explosion of public commemorative events in post-bellum America served to reinforce the experience of a century as a "natural" rhythm, just as the pace of modern life quickened so that a hundred years would bring greater changes than ever before.

In the reckoning of historical change, the rhythm of a century is wholly arbitrary, an artifact of a human mathematical system, and yet, as stated above, there is hidden within it an intuition of its symmetry with the single year in the life of an individual—taking the birth of Jesus of Nazareth as the starting point. The key to this symmetry was revealed by Rudolf Steiner:

> All of the actions of former generations, all the impulses and the deeds connected with them, pour into historical evolution and have a life cycle of 33 years. Then comes the Easter time of these deeds and impulses, the time of resurrection.... All things in historical evolution are transfigured after 33 years, arise as from the grave, by virtue of a power connected with the holiest of all redemptions, the Mystery of Golgotha.... Just as we calculate the cyclic rotations of celestial bodies so we must learn to calculate historic events by means of a true science of history....

"33" was Rudolf Steiner's shorthand for 33⅓, for the historical law that Steiner suggests here is a consequence of the actual biography of Jesus Christ, whose life—from the birth of Jesus of Nazareth on the night of December 6/7, 2 BC, to the Resurrection at sunrise on Easter Sunday morning, April 5, AD 33—lasted 12,173⅓ days, or 33.329 years, which is 33⅓ years less 1½ days. Rudolf Steiner pointed out that, in addition to the various planetary rhythms (the one-year rhythm of the Sun; 29½–year rhythm of Saturn; 12–year rhythm of Jupiter, and so on), since the moment of Christ's resurrection, the 33⅓–year rhythm of the life of Christ Jesus has become of signal importance to the unfolding of human history.

This is where the popular acceptance of the century as an increment worthy of celebration overlaps with this esoteric truth: the rhythm of 33⅓ years occurs almost exactly three times in one century. Since the rhythm is a day and a half less than 33⅓ years, the "commemoration" of any event migrates slightly backwards in time. If one follows this rhythm, the third cycle—the second since Christ's death and resurrection—completes at sunset on December

1, AD 99. Following this rhythm through the centuries, one arrives at the threshold of the twentieth century at the completion of the 57th cycle, on September 10, 1899. This rhythm was intuited by the millennia-old Hindu historical calendar that set the end of the 5000-year-long Kali Yuga in 1899.

Like Rudolf Steiner, Henry Adams felt a need for a "true science of history." In his 1909 essay, "The Rule of Phase Applied to History," he sought a "social physics" where historical change could be plotted as exactly as physics could predict the instant of phase change in substances like water. Indeed, Adams drew his inspiration from Josiah Gibbs, whose 1903 paper, "On the Equilibrium of Heterogeneous Substances," laid the foundation for much of modern thermodynamics. Reeling from the "doubling rate" of historical change occasioned by modern technology, Adams felt he had discovered the formula for determining divisions of time in the past, and for extrapolating into the future. He argued that a new "mechanical" phase had begun in 1600 with the thought of Galileo, Bacon, and Descartes, and that this had lasted 300 years, until the "electric" phase, marked by the invention of the dynamo. Applying the law of inverse squares, the electrical phase would have a life of $\sqrt{300}$—about 17 years. Thus Adams, drawing on a very different meaning than Steiner's "etheric," anticipated that the "ethereal" phase—the phase of pure mathematics—would begin around 1917. At the opening of the twentieth century, Adams found History gasping for breath, and saw proof of the looming entropic heat death of society in Gustav Le Bon's *The Psychology of Crowds*, which portrayed the modern urban dweller as a "savage . . . with all his momentary violence."

MANHATTAN

Such a gloomy theory found no purchase at Manhattan's Hudson-Fulton Celebration. In fact, the planners quickly embraced the notion of a historical parade as the main method of teaching history to "the crowd." Rejecting the idea of a historical pageant as too exclusive, since admission would have to be charged, the Historical and Carnival Parades Committee hired A.H. Stoddard, veteran Master of the Mardi Gras parades in New Orleans, to organize, design, and build the floats for the Hudson-Fulton Celebration. After renting a pair of buildings on the Harlem River in the Bronx to serve as a workshop (called, after New Orleans fashion, "the Den"), Stoddard brought a crew of skilled workers up from the Big Easy, and they supervised a group of 160 designers, modelers, papier-mâché workers, carpenters, painters, decorators, costume makers, and watchmen, patrolling day and night on the lookout for fire or other dangers. From imitation flames and cabbages to heroic figures of men and women, and life-sized models of horses and cows, to an eagle standing eight feet tall, with a wingspan of fifteen feet, a city of papier-mâché inhabitants grew inside the shop.

One hundred and four floats carried the figures on a six-mile procession down Central Park West to Central Park South, to Fifth Avenue, and then on to Washington Square. Headed by a platoon of mounted New York City policemen and Mayor George B. McClellan, there followed on foot a dozen highly decorated members of the Hudson-Fulton Celebration Commission, including Captain Cornelius Vanderbilt. A 100-piece marching band rounded them out, and then followed the First Division: 400 men of the Friendly Sons of St. Patrick; 2600 men of the Ancient Order of Hibernians; 1500 from the Italian Societies; another 1500 from the Bohemian Societies; 250 each from the Polish, Hungarians, and Norwegians. Marching bands accompanied each of the ethnic societies. A 25-piece "Red Man Band" followed, and then a series of floats illustrating New York's "Indian Period." The "Legend of Hiawatha" float bore a canoe in whose prow stood Hiawatha, while nearby, a maiden lay crushed to death by the giant eagle, depicting the moment before, according to legend, Hiawatha formed the League of the Iroquois. Atotarho, the serpent-maned Onondaga chief, rode in the next float, seated amid bulrushes, surrounded by snakes and frogs, while approached by Indians bearing propitiatory offerings. Other floats showed Indians: manufacturing implements of "war and the chase"; hunting; dancing to appease the "Great Spirit, that he might mitigate the rigors of winter, which at one time killed many Indians"; and an Indian war dance. Seventy Iroquois men, women and children played themselves on the floats, but over a thousand members of the Improved Order of Red Men and the

Society of Tammany joined them. None of the Historical Commit-
tee seemed to have been aware that Manhattan was home to the
Lenape people, not Iroquois; "Manhattan" is from *menahen*, the
Lenape word for "island."

Next came the floats portraying the "Dutch Period": beginning
with a float bearing a papier-mâché reproduction of the *Half Moon*,
and another showing "The Fate of Henry Hudson"—the float
showed Hudson adrift in a lifeboat in Hudson's Bay in 1611, with
two polar bears on an iceberg; there followed the purchase of Manhattan Island; Jonas Bronck's 1642 treaty with the Indians; the
reception of Peter Stuyvesant; bowling on the Bowling Green; and
Saint Nicholas. The "Colonial Period" floats included a scene of
Col. Peter Schuyler at St. James Palace in London with a party of
five Iroquois chiefs; the trial of John Peter Zenger; the Stamp Act;
the destruction of the statue of King George in 1776; the storming of
Stony Point; and the capture of Major André; George Washington
taking the oath of office. Floats representing Washington Irving's
legends of Rip van Winkle and Sleepy Hollow carried up the rear.

The "United States and Modern Period" opened with a scale
reproduction of the *Clermont*, then moved on to the reception of
Lafayette in 1824; an Erie Canal boat; an old Broadway sleigh; the
introduction of Croton Reservoir water; the Statue of Liberty, and
again closing with a Washington Irving tale, a float showing Father
Knickerbocker welcoming to New York City all those coming from
foreign lands.

This tendency of myth and folklore to keep intruding into History was even more pronounced in the "Carnival Parade," which
took place on the last Saturday of the Celebration:

> This feature of the Celebration was adopted with a serious as
> well as festive purpose . . . the Carnival Pageant illustrated that
> great body of Old World folklore which has inspired so much
> of the beautiful imagery of poetry, song and drama of all civi-
> lized nations. Although the legends and allegories represented
> were not indigenous to America, yet they form a real part of
> our culture, inherited, like the cumulative facts which consti-
> tute our progressive civilization, from the past.

The "Music, Literature, and Art" title car heading the procession was in the shape of a fantastic dragon spouting flames. Mars followed, riding his papier-mâché chariot in the clouds, and after him came a dozen floats with scenes drawn from Richard Wagner's operas—*Lohengrin*, *The Ring of the Nibelungen*, *Tannhauser*, and *The Mastersingers of Nuremberg*. Floats for Titania—the Fairy Queen of Shakespeare's *Midsummer Night's Dream*—and the Frost King were bedecked with women in winged gossamer outfits playing fairies. Andromeda, Diana, Europa, Medusa, and the Sirens brought in Greek mythology, before this section of the parade ended with "Gnomes," "Elves of the Spring," and "Good Luck"—which had a horseshoe, rabbit, four-leafed clover, black cat and other bearers of good and bad luck backed by a massive drapery bearing the Swastika, universal symbol of good fortune.

The Carnival Parade did not repeat the Historical Parade's pretense at a continuous narrative, and yet the concluding floats uncannily expressed the deepest layers of the city's psyche. Float # 44 was a scene of sexy mermaids cavorting at the bottom of the sea; Float #45 showed fairies at play with butterflies; Float #46 captured the moment when the Prince discovered Cinderella's slipper; in Float #47, Orpheus played his lyre before Pluto. The final float sported Uncle Sam receiving the crown heads of Europe. For all of the bluster about "progress," the collective unconscious of the great island city kept regressing into juvenile, oceanic fantasies.

BURLINGTON

It had been the same in Burlington in July, where the most memorable images carried away by the crowd mixed superficial stereotypes of the mythic past with the fantastic present of modernity. During the last moment of the Tercentenary week, at the fireworks display that followed the pageants, an otherworldly atmosphere was created. According to the *Burlington Free Press*:

> Spectators at the grandstand on the lakeshore might have fancied they were in a veritable fairyland last evening with the brilliant pyrotechnical displays multiplied many times in the ripples of the surface of the lake, the flitting lights of the boats,

the illumination of the Lake Champlain Yacht Club. . . . The performance was preceded by a military band concert, the sharp yip, yip and cries of the Indians who were dancing about on the large raft under the glowing electric arc lights, giving a wild and weird tinge to the music. This, with the reflection of the many lights on the water, the stars twinkling in the heavens, the lights of many yachts glistening, and the ink black background made a scene to be remembered. . . .

The fireworks represented a powerful technology of communal fantasy, bringing together a large and diverse and often polarized community in an incredible spectacle of light and dark. For at least a moment, when the last few rockets hung in the sky over the lake, ten thousand people were silent. Then they burst into a chorus of cheers as the rockets exploded. There seemed to be complete union in the warm July dark.

The next morning, as city workers cleared confetti from the sidewalks, newsboys hawked the morning edition. The front page had a story about Barre stonecutter Regina Rizieri, who lost the thumb and two fingers of his left hand to a firecracker. There were also stories of a Poughkeepsie, New York boy who had tried to see if he could smother the sound of a firecracker; when it exploded, it set the boy's clothes on fire and burned him to death. Another boy on a dare held a firecracker in his mouth and blew out all of his teeth. Other news that morning seemed little different from ordinary mornings. July 1st' s front page had a graphic round-by-round description of the Stanley Ketchel/Billy Papke fight in San Francisco: "The feature of the fight was the extreme viciousness with which both men fought and the apparent hatred that lurked behind every blow." July 7th's paper juxtaposed these stories: in the left-hand column, "Frenchmen Honor Their Countrymen" described the Tercentenary addresses in French by priests from St. Hyacinthe, Quebec; in the right column, "International Celebration Now" reported on the arrival of President Taft and the British, French, and Japanese prime ministers. In between these two columns were the dissonant notes of "An Attempted Assassination," about Beatrix Thompson of Burlington, an anti-Catholic woman who the day before had taken a shot at Father Gillis as he walked up Loomis Street to St. Mary's Academy to say mass for the nuns. She had put a hole in his umbrella, but missed him. In the next column, "Boy Killed by an Automobile" told how Hector Mongeon of St. Hyacinthe (one of the boys from the choir that sang at the Tercentenary celebration) was riding down College Street on his bicycle when a car hit him and sped off. The next day the driver was apprehended—William Benware, Governor Prouty's chauffeur. Witnesses identified the vehicle by its license plate—"1909." Hector Mongeon was the first person ever to be killed by an automobile in Burlington. All this took place the day before the part of the Tercentenary celebration that would see Burlington's largest automobile parade ever.

Out at the lot on South Winooski Avenue, a few thousand people gathered to watch the launch of the mammoth airship. As the crowd jockeyed for position, one man bumped into Burlington policeman Bruno Riley, who hit the man twice in the face with his billy club. The assembled crowd was about to rip Riley apart when Mayor John Burke, who was there to give a speech, intervened. When the airship was finally launched, its propeller ripped a huge gash in the silk balloon and it dropped back to earth.

To add to the magic of the floats in the Hudson-Fulton Celebration Carnival Parade, the organizers had arranged for extensive burning along the parade route of "colored fire," a pyrotechnic effect that produced billowing clouds of rainbow-hued smoke. The colored clouds enveloped the leeward-side spectators, irritating their eyes and lungs, and sent them fleeing from the grandstands in search of clear air.

If the Etheric Christ was really coming in the clouds, He was going to meet quite a bit of turbulence.

3

MEPHISTOPHELEAN
MURMURS

BY DUSK ON THE INAUGURAL EVENING of the Hudson-Fulton celebration, the war fleet had made a midstream line up the Hudson
for ten miles, from 42nd Street to Spuyten Duyvil Creek on the
north. The ships were eerily quiet, their presence revealed to the
mass of spectators only by their faint silhouettes and an occasional
signal flashed from ship to ship. Then, at the sound of eight bells,
the entire fleet

> burst into outlines of light, as if suddenly touched with the pro-
> pitious augury of St. Elmo's fire—the masts, decks, water lines
> and other chief features glowing with thousands of sparkling
> electric globes. And for hours these ponderous, death-dealing
> machines, lying peacefully on the bosom of the Hudson in
> friendly association, scintillated like the airy fabrics of a magi-
> cian or the unsubstantial dreams of an oriental fairy tale. It was
> a scene of exquisite beauty which will never be forgotten by the
> millions of people who thronged to the river side to see it.

The plan was for this surprise illumination to be augmented by a
massive fireworks display that had been set up on four floats
anchored at intervals of 1000 feet along the New Jersey shore
directly across from Riverside Park. Just after the fireworks began,
as the crowd watched, the floats were cut loose from their moorings
and drifted downriver. That evening the telegraph operators were
reporting problems with their lines, and it was attributed to the fireworks operation, since the floats were very close to their telegraph
cable crossing the river.

New York City telegraph operators were not the only ones having trouble with their lines. Since dawn that morning, telegraph service all over the world had been disrupted. Calling it an "aurora"—since they knew from experience that brilliant displays of the northern lights typically followed such disturbances—telegraph operators wrestled with the strange force, which peaked at about noon, but then continued to 'throb' in the afternoon and evening. Wires would go dead for a few moments, pick up slowly, and then die again. Telephone systems were useless as well. New York City, with the nation's densest grid of electrical communications, was most severely affected, but the pulsing wave of electromagnetic energy moved steadily westward, knocking out telegraph service in Cincinnati, Chicago, and beyond, all the way to Seattle and San Francisco. Instruments in telegraph offices measured a current of 500 volts in the atmosphere—greater voltage than was usually supplied along the lines. In western Australia, from Perth to Kalgoorlie, a distance of 350 miles, the line kept operating for a half hour even though the batteries had been disconnected. Incandescent lamps attached to the wires lit up from the atmospheric electricity, and brilliant sparks flashed across the gaps whenever operators opened their telegraph keys. Reports from around the world the next day showed that the aurora borealis was seen generally as far south as 30° North Latitude, but Jakarta and Singapore—at 1° North and 6° South—had also experienced the aurora.

The presumption by the telegraph company that the fireworks might have been the cause of the problem suggests how new and mysterious electromagnetism was, even a half century after the first telegraph lines were strung across America. Newspaper reports discussed the theory that the magnetic storm was caused by sunspots as just one of a number of competing theories. At the time of the September 25 storm, Guglielmo Marconi was in New York, and when the *New York Times* asked him for his explanation, he said that sunspots might have little to do with it. He did, however, gloat over the fact that his new wireless telegraph was not as adversely affected as standard telegraph systems were by the auroral storm. "I can't help being a little glad the telegraph companies have had this object lesson," Marconi told the *Times.*

The sky was full of all manner of signs and wonders in 1909. Underneath the Marconi interview in the *Times*, a tiny filler item from the newswire noted that in Hawaii on the 25th, there had been "a display of fireworks of the most spectacular sort"—attributed to a meteor shower. But in recent months there had been stranger sightings—a report of an hour-long storm of hot globular rain in Santa Cruz, California; a meteor that had dropped through the roof of a house in Texas, and other meteorites from New Jersey and Massachusetts and Connecticut and Mexico City. A brief survey of article titles from the very sober journal, *The English Mechanic*, gives a fair picture of Brittania's skies around 1909: "Glorious Midnight Sky"; "Smoke-Like Darkness Before the Storm"; "Aurora"; "Nocturnal Glows"; "Nocturnal Northern Glows"; "Curious Lunar Observation"; "Electrical Fireballs"; "Unexplained Ringing of House Bells"; "Globular Lightning"; "Ball Lightning". In May and June, there were scattered reports of a wave of phantom airship sightings —the twentieth century's first "UFOs"—from all over Great Britain. In July and August, thousands of New Zealanders observed zeppelin-type ships, and then in late August, they were sighted on the east coast of Australia.

It was no wonder then, that in December, when reports of mysterious airships began to pour in from various places in New England, that the press reasoned that the sightings were of a still secret flying machine being tested by its inventor. On the 20th of December, immigration inspector Arthur Hoe reported seeing an airship flying rapidly through the clear night sky over Boston. On the 22nd, in Worcester, more than two thousand people watched as a flying machine circled in the southeast for over three hours. A crowd of Christmas shoppers and a number of police officers then watched as the lighted airship sailed over the city, stopping for a few minutes over the State Mutual Life Insurance building. According to the *Times* article, hundreds of reports came in from neighboring Massachusetts towns of Marlboro, Cambridge, Revere, Greendale, Nahant, Maynard, Fitchburg, Leominster, and Westboro, and many of these viewers talked to each other by telephone as they watched the ship.

The following day, when the mystery vessel appeared again over Worcester, fifty thousand residents poured into the streets, bringing the city to a standstill. The *Times* reprinted the *Boston Globe*'s report: "In the main thoroughfare people with bundles stood agape. Men and boys poured from clubrooms and women rushed from the houses to view this phenomenon. The streets were thronged." On Christmas Eve, there were thirty-three reports, from every New England state. One article reported: "On the streets the greeting wasn't 'Merry Christmas.' It was 'Did you see it?'"

Up until this point, only a single article ever suggested that the sightings were in error—a *Times* editorial hinted sarcastically about New Englanders' having historically had a penchant for witchcraft trials. But then, on December 27, when six more sightings were reported, all the newspapers voiced skepticism, frequently invoking Venus as the real cause of the sightings. A *Globe* reporter said Marlboro was "airship crazy." The headline in the *Providence Journal* read "CITY IS AIRSHIP MAD." Newspaper editors began to attribute the sightings to a sort of mass hysteria: "The epidemic of infected vision that has turned Massachusetts upside down struck town with a bang late yesterday afternoon...." A week before the newspapers had all been covering the appearance of a marvelous new flying craft; now they were without exception aggressively uncovering a hoax. Journalists lampooned colleagues who gave credibility to any sightings, saying that they had a vested interest in keeping the story alive as a way of selling newspapers. "WILLIMANTIC MEN SEE THINGS AGAIN" and "WILLIMANTIC VICTIM OF AIRSHIP FAKING" blasted the headlines from the *Hartford Courant*.

A million people had watched Wilbur Wright fly a very real airplane up the Hudson in broad daylight just two months before; airships were all the rage, but newspaper editors and reporters—the same ones who fell over themselves getting stories and photographs documenting the latest in aviation news—could without pause dismiss their readers as credulous, and attribute all the excitement to an episode of wishful thinking. In 1909, newspapers had already succeeded in undermining the authority of the eyewitness. A steady diet of telegraphed, instantaneous "news" erased not only traditional democratic notions of authority, but also fostered a kind of collective amnesia. One needed only glance over newspapers a couple of months old to glean arcana that fleshed out the aerial enigma a bit further.

In Willimantic, the town that had so recently become a laughing-stock, there had been in late October another sky mystery. At 12:35 AM on the 22nd, residents heard a heavy peal of thunder, and saw a ball of fire descend from the sky. In the neighboring town of Storrs, home to the State Agricultural College, two men—one of them the football coach—watched as the sizzling fireball, trailing a 40-foot-long tail, streaked over a dairy barn and struck a telephone pole in front of Beebe's General Store, splintering and twisting the pole before entering a nearby house at ground level and then exiting from an upper story. Inside, Mr. F. M. Chadwick and his family were thrown out of their beds, and found that the fireball had torn off baseboard, broken glass, and made dozens of holes in his ceilings—without ever setting the house on fire. A scientist from the college came out the next day to look over the damage, which included four or five huge holes in Mr. Chadwick's front yard, but could only say that it was "some terrific force."

During the December airship episode, Baltic, Connecticut resi-dent P. D. Donahue stated he could discern two men in the vessel as it passed by. But this simple observation paled in comparison to eyewitness reports earlier that year from Great Britain and New Zealand. On the 18th of May, in Cardiff, Wales, a Mr. Lithbridge had been walking around 11 PM along a road near the Caerphilly Moun-tains, when he spied off in the grass a large, tubular construction. When he approached it, he found two men inside, in heavy fur overcoats. Seeing Mr. Lithbridge, they spoke to each other in some foreign tongue, and then flew off. In January 1910, the vicar, the mayor and some policemen of Invercargill, New Zealand, spotted a cigar-shaped object hovering about 100 feet off the ground. As they watched it, a man appeared at a side door and shouted to them in an unknown language, before the craft shot out of sight.

1909, the *annus mirabilis* for the history of the Hudson and Champlain Valley, was also an *annus mirabilis* for skywatchers. But then again, so was 1908 a year of aerial oddities. At the time of the solar eclipse of June 28, 1908, visible across the northeastern United States, a great luminous object was seen (the *Times* reported the day before the eclipse that it would not get much attention from local scientists, since they were out of the city vacationing). In July there were reports from locations scattered across New England—Bristol, Connecticut; Pittsfield, Massachusetts; White River Junction, Vermont—of strange bright sky objects. The most spectacular sky event of 1908 occurred over the Tunguska River region of Siberia, on June 30, when some unnamed object exploded above the earth with a force 1000 times greater than the Hiroshima atomic bomb. The explosion incinerated trees within a 9-mile radius of the explosion's epicenter, and leveled trees over a 25-mile radius. It is estimated that some 80 million trees were destroyed, over an area of 830 square miles. Peasants in the tiny village of Korelina were so stunned by the crashes that they sent a representative to the local archpriest to ask if the end of the world was beginning, and how they were preparing for it in the bigger village of Kirensk. Over the next few weeks, in far-flung places all over the world, night skies were aglow such that one could read in their light. In the United States, the Smithsonian Astrophysical Observatory and the Mount Wilson Observatory observed a decrease in atmospheric transparency that lasted for several months.

Although newspapers in towns some distance from the explosion gave eyewitness reports soon after the event, only in 1921 was there a scientific investigation, when Russian mineralogist Leonid Kulik visited the explosion site. On a subsequent expedition in 1930, Kulik recorded this testimony from a man living about 40 miles south of where the explosion took place:

> At breakfast time I was sitting by the house at Vanavara trading post, facing North.... I suddenly saw that directly to the North, over Onkoul's Tunguska road, the sky split in two and fire appeared high and wide over the forest. The split in the sky grew larger, and the entire Northern side was covered with fire. At that moment I became so hot that I couldn't bear it, as if my shirt was on fire; from the northern side, where the fire was, came strong heat. I wanted to tear off my shirt and throw it down, but then the sky shut closed, and a strong thump sounded, and I was thrown a few yards. I lost my senses for a

moment, but then my wife ran out and led me to the house. After that such noise came, as if rocks were falling or cannons were firing, the earth shook, and when I was on the ground, I pressed my head down, fearing rocks would smash it. When the sky opened up, hot wind raced between the houses, like from cannons, which left traces in the ground like pathways, and it damaged some crops. Later we saw that many windows were shattered, and in the barn a part of the iron lock snapped.

Contemporary accounts almost invariably speak as if there were a single object responsible for the explosion at Tunguska, but eyewitnesses clearly agree that there were several bright objects in the sky, following different trajectories, moving at different speeds, sometimes stopping or changing course, as if the objects were maneuvering. Eyewitnesses frequently spoke of a "second sun" appearing in the sky, accompanied by earthquakes, rumbling, or other noises. A man from Moga, a village about 185 miles from the center of the explosion, said that this second sun's light "stripped the world of its familiar, pleasant shapes. Everything, from the smallest blade of grass to the cedar tree, suddenly seemed different from how it had always been. Colors vanished; so did the usual three-dimensionality of the world, warmth, tenderness. Our world had gone. . . ."

A number of observers closest to the site reported shafts of light appearing from *out of the earth*. At the nearby Stepanovsky coal mine, miners felt an earthquake about 30 minutes before the explosion, then, as they heard a tremendous roar and hum, the waters in a small lake dropped away, just before a column of light rose from the bottom of the depression. In the 1960s, an elderly Evenk (formerly the natives of this region were called the "Tungus") man—said to have been a shaman who had been hiding from the Soviet authorities for decades—gave his story of the explosion. He had been hunting along the Chamba River, about 25 miles from the epicenter:

> [the sky] was all falling around me, burning. You don't think that was god flying, it was really devil flying. I lift up my head and see devils flying. The devil itself was like a billet, light color, two eyes in front, fire behind. I was frightened, covered myself . . . prayed (not to the heathen god, I prayed to Jesus

Christ and Virgin Mary). After some time of prayer I recovered: everything was clear.

There is no reason that one should link the Tunguska explosion with the explosion that occurred in downtown Burlington on July 2, 1907. But let us consider it. Slightly before noon, directly above the intersection of Church and College Streets, residents heard a loud explosion, and rushed into the street to see what had happened. They found a horse lying flat in the street in front of the Standard Coal and Ice Company's office. Thinking the horse had been struck and killed by lightning, a moment later the animal rose to its feet.

Former Governor of Vermont Urban Woodbury and Bishop John Michaud were talking at the corner of Church and College when the explosion occurred. Governor Woodbury, who had been facing in the direction of the lake, turned round suddenly, expecting to see bricks flying through the air. Facing east up College Street, Bishop Michaud saw a ball of fire rushing through the air just east of the National Biscuit Company building. Groceryman Alvaro Adsit also saw the ball of fire, and a young man looking out of a window in the Strong Theater said he saw the ball strike the center of College Street near the coal company office, knocking the horse down before bounding back up into the sky. Moments later, though the sky had been completely clear, there was a downpour of rain that lasted half an hour.

A week later, Burlington's weather forecaster William H. Alexander wrote up a report of the event based on his interviews with eyewitnesses. The weatherman—in this inland maritime town a much respected figure given the importance of his prognostications for the until recently booming lake shipping trade—put it all down to a case of "ball lightning": "Without doubt this is one of the most unusual electrical phenomena known to me. The 'explosion' was so sudden, so unexpected, that it startled practically the entire city. There was a general, spontaneous rush to the window or street to see what had happened." Alvaro Adsit described how he had been standing in his store and was looking north when he noticed a yellowish "ball of fire" about ten inches across fall to a point on the other side of the street, exploding with a deafening noise. Banker

W. P. Dodds saw the "ball" just before the explosion and confirmed the details given by Adsit and Bishop Michaud.

Bishop Michaud told Alexander that he had seen a torpedo-shaped body about 300 feet away, suspended in the air about 50 feet above the tops of the buildings. About six feet long by eight inches in diameter, the dark object had tongues of red flame projecting from it, and after remaining stationary for some moments, moved slowly off over Dolan Brothers Store at the corner of College and Mechanic Streets. Bishop Michaud commented on a halo of dim light, some 20 feet in diameter, that enveloped the odd object, and said that the downpour which followed the object's appearance issued from a cloudless sky. The Bishop was obviously shaken by the experience: "Four weeks have passed since the occurrence of this event, but the picture of that scene and the terrific concussion caused by it, are vividly before me, while the crashing sound still rings in my ears. I hope I may never see or hear a similar phenomenon, at least at such close range."

A century after the Tunguska and Burlington explosions, both remain complete mysteries. Considerable scientific effort has been directed toward explaining the Tunguska event, while the Burlington event has been merely an item of UFO folklore, thanks to Charles Fort having included it in his *Book of the Damned* (1919). The book is a stunning survey of the "Super-Sargasso Sea," the hyper-dimension suspended somewhere between Earth and Heaven, from which issued all manner of inexplicable phenomena, from falls of blood and fish to fairy stones and exploding torpedo-shaped intrusions. At the time of the Burlington and Tunguska explosions, as well as the September 25, 1909 auroral event, it is likely that Fort was sitting in the reading room of the New York Public Library, his home away from home for more than ten years, where he scrupulously pored over major metropolitan newspapers; prestigious scientific journals; and obscure meteorological missives, in his quest to get to the bottom of those phenomena that had been "damned" by modern materialist science.

Fort's use of "damned" showed considerable epistemological sophistication, for despite his mischievous sense of play upon every page of *Book of the Damned*, the book was a serious—and still completely unanswered—challenge to the scientific establishment. In a sense, Fort's work anticipated by half a century the philosophical iconoclasm of Thomas Kuhn. While Kuhn and his successors employ dense academic jargon in their critique, Fort goes right for the jugular, and unlike Kuhn, he is unafraid to let his curiosity and skepticism take him absolutely *anywhere*, including into the Plutonic realm of the truly "damned," in more than just a modern philosophical sense. In Chapter 6 of *Book of the Damned*, Fort itemizes a dazzling array of episodes of precipitating slag and cinders and ash and coal and other "carbonaceous substances" from round the world, and then he dances with the devilish brimstone:

> The fall of sulphur from the sky has been especially repulsive to the modern orthodoxy—largely because of its associations with the superstitions or principles of the preceding orthodoxy—stories of devils: sulphurous exhalations. Several writers have said that they have had this feeling. So the scientific reactionists, who have rabidly fought the preceding, because it was the preceding: and the scientific prudes, who, in sheer exclusionism, have held lean hands over pale eyes, denying falls of sulphur. I have many notes upon the sulphurous odor of meteorites, and many notes upon phosphorescence of things that come from externality. Some day I shall look over old stories of demons that have appeared sulphurously upon this earth, with the idea of expressing that we have often had undesirable visitors from other worlds; or that an indication of external derivation is sulphurousness. I expect some day to rationalize demonology, but just at present we are scarcely far enough advanced to go so far back.

The only place that one could find demons in the Champlain and Hudson historical celebrations was in the midst of the floating pageant island's brief depiction of Iroquois magic, or the Carnival Parade's Atotarho float. Modern America had banished, "damned" these, as outmoded specters of the human imagination, long ago abandoning whatever thin demonology might have been possessed by such sterling representatives of Henry Adams's "mechanical phase" as Samuel de Champlain or Henry Hudson.

January 1, 1909: Berlin

On the morning of the first day of 1909, someone had passed a note to Rudolf Steiner asking for an esoteric explanation of earthquakes, particularly whether they could be foreseen by clairvoyance, and why, if this was so, no warnings would be given. The questioner had been stirred to ask the question in light of the tragic earthquake in Messina, Sicily on December 28th, which early reports estimated to have killed over 100,000 people. Lasting less than a minute, the tremor and resulting 40-foot high tsunami wave destroyed 90% of the buildings in Messina. It was the most devastating earthquake ever to hit Europe. When Rudolf Steiner lectured that evening, he spoke of earthquakes in only the last ten minutes, but clearly, the entire lecture was an answer to the listener's question. Steiner began by speaking about the figure of Mephistopheles from Goethe's *Faust*, quoting Mephistopheles as saying: ""Sink then! I might as well say, Mount!/'Tis quite the same." By way of this quote, Steiner takes up immediately Fort's dilemma of the "Super-Sargasso Sea," showing that in Mephistopheles' realm, there is no difference between "below" and "above." Pointing out that the Hebrew *mephiz* means "one who obstructs, who corrupts," and *topel* means "one who lies," Steiner characterizes Mephistopheles as "a spirit of untruth, deception and illusion," and then asks directly: "Who is Mephistopheles, in reality?"

After stating at length what Mephistopheles is *not*—Lucifer— Steiner identified him with the adversarial being of the Sun Spirit *Ahura Mazdao*, whom Zarathustra taught the Persian civilization to know as *Angra Mainyu*, or "Ahriman". Ahriman/Mephistopheles had been known under many different names to the peoples of the past, but in European civilization he was Satan, the Devil. While Lucifer influences beings in the astral realm, Ahriman controls the beings of the etheric, and is able to take control of human beings who engage in black magical training or who were prone to abnormal somnambulistic states. Steiner often spoke of the dangers of these states in hypnotism and Spiritualism, which were still gaining adherents in the twentieth century. Just a few weeks after the Hudson-Fulton celebration, Eusapia Palladino, the Italian 'physical

medium' whose spectacular paranormal productions—material-
izing phantom limbs; playing musical instruments at a distance;
moving furniture and other objects with her mind—had for twenty
years been studied by scientists from all over Europe, arrived in
New York to submit to the poking and prodding of its skeptical scientists. Palladino was an example of just the kind of "somnambu-
lant" that Steiner warned against, that is, in her production of
physical phenomena through the diminishing of her own Ego consciousness, Palladino opened the door to malevolent, harmful Ahrimanic spiritual beings.

Steiner predicted both that "the civilization immediately to come
will see the appearance of many things connected with Ahriman's
influence," and that protection against Ahriman would steadily
diminish, as "many signs proclaim it—our epoch courts these influences of Ahriman." Though he said nothing explicitly about what
these signs were, the implicit suggestion was that the most spectacular sign was earthquakes, including the Messina quake. While
Lucifer worked in the elements of air and water, Ahriman's activity,
Steiner said, was within the elements of earth and fire, meaning by
this the *etheric* realms of earth and fire. Tectonic activity—including
earthquakes and volcanoes—registered the effect of Ahriman's
activity within those etheric realms. Within the nine etheric sublev-
els of the Earth—the "Tartarus" of Greek mythology—Ahriman
operated from the sixth layer, the "Fire Earth," which Steiner also
called the "Passion Earth," identifying it as a highly sensitive zone
that reacts to human excesses of will and outbreaks of passion.

Though Christ had "cast Ahriman into fetters" through the Mystery of Golgotha, Ahriman's influence remained in the form of
materialistic human thinking. Inwardly connecting to the Christ
was the sole path in the present to resisting Ahriman. Steiner made
it clear that *all* of humanity was destined to confront the powers of
Ahriman, but certain places on the earth were more susceptible to
the stirrings of Ahriman and the Fire Earth than others. Steiner
made it clear that the people who lived in the regions that suffered
devastating earthquakes were not necessarily the cause of these
catastrophes; they were produced through the deeds and thoughts
of *all* human beings. A massive international relief effort—one of

the first ever—was underway to help the people of the Messina region, and Steiner wished in no way to discourage this effort:

> These catastrophes were evoked by the collective karma of humanity.... Our volcanic eruptions and earthquakes are nothing else than the echoes of these catastrophes. But it should never so much as occur to anyone to attach an iota of guilt to the victim of such a calamity or to withhold compassion in the fullest measure. It must be absolutely clear to an anthroposophist that the karma of these individuals has nothing to do with the guilt to which the catastrophes are due and it should never occur to him to withhold help from anyone because—to put it trivially—he believes in karma and therefore assumes that this destiny was brought on by the man himself.

At the very end of his lecture, Steiner came round to the question of prediction, and said that only two or three times a century was it permitted by the spiritual world for initiates to speak out from their foreknowledge of an earthquake or other nature catastrophe. Like all of the great spiritual teachers of history, Rudolf Steiner always knew a great deal more than he ever said, and throughout his life as a teacher, he continually planted seeds for future students to take up and nurture toward new growth. For all that he did say in this lecture and a couple of others about the subterranean region of the Earth, he seemed here to be leaving open for future research the question of how exactly Ahriman's relationship to the Fire Earth might manifest in the present.

Without realizing it, Charles Fort took up at least one aspect of this question—with his usual irreverent gusto. In *Book of the Damned*, after chapters puzzling over precipitations from the Super-Sargasso Sea of: erratic comets; oddly shaped and inscribed "thunderstones"; stone-chucking poltergeists; sulphurous stuff of varying size and texture; "angel hair" and other homogeneous masses of fibrous or gelatinous substances; and a litany of creatures—fish, frogs, snakes, worms, etc.—Fort comes to a "pseudo-conclusion":

> That we've been damned by giants sound asleep, or by great scientific principles and abstractions that cannot realize them-

selves; that little harlots have visited their caprices upon us; that clowns, with buckets of water from which they pretend to cast thousands of good-sized fishes have anathematized us for laughing disrespectfully, because, as with all clowns, underlying buffoonery is the desire to be taken seriously; that pale ignorances, presiding over microscopes by which they cannot distinguish flesh from nostoc or fishes' spawn or frogs' spawn, have visited upon us their wan solemnities. We've been damned by corpses and skeletons and mummies, which twitch and totter with pseudo-life derived from conveniences.

And then he continues, pressing on into new territories of anomalous phenomena. Over the years, he developed a special penchant for "extracurricular" aspects of earthquakes. He mapped out four classes of phenomena that precede or accompany earthquakes: unusual clouds; profound darkness (during daylight hours); luminous appearances in the sky; and falls of substances and objects commonly called "meteorites"—but obviously *not*. Here is just a small sampling of Fort's pre-1840 itinerary of concurrence of aerial phenomena associated with earthquakes:

Earthquake "preceded" by a violent tempest, England, Jan. 8, 1704—"preceded" by a brilliant meteor, Switzerland, Nov. 4, 1704—"luminous cloud, moving at high velocity, disappearing behind the horizon," Florence, Dec. 9, 1731—"thick mists in the air, through which a dim light was seen: several weeks before the shock, globes of fire had been seen in the air," Swabia, May 28, 1732—rain of earth, Carpentras, France, Oct. 18, 1737—a black cloud, London, March 19, 1750—violent storm and a strange star of octagonal shape, Slavenge, Norway, April 15, 1752—balls of fire from a streak in the sky, Augermannland, 1752—numerous meteorites, Lisbon, Oct. 15, 1755—"terrible tempests" over and over—"falls of hail" and "brilliant meteors," instance after instance—"an immense globe," Switzerland, Nov. 2, 1761—oblong, sulphurous cloud, Germany, April, 1767—extraordinary mass of vapor, Bologna, April, 1780—heavens obscured by a dark mist, Grenada, Aug. 7, 1804—"strange howling noises in the air, and large spots obscuring the sun," Palermo, Italy, April 16, 1817—"luminous meteor moving in the same direction as that taken by the shock," Naples, Nov. 22, 1821—fire ball appearing in the sky: apparent size of the moon, Thuringerwald, Nov. 29, 1831.

Fort emphasized that not a single one of these events had a place within the principles of modern seismology. They were truly *"damned."*

Without ever naming it so, Fort was retrospectively inventorying "signs of the times," at a moment—the turn of the twentieth century—when sightings of "ball lightning" and other luminous phenomena, whether or not at the time of earthquakes, were increasingly giving way to reports of airships bearing bright searchlights, capable of unheard of speeds, and sometimes even operated by small men speaking in strange tongues. Though he died a decade before the first "little green men" and "flying saucers," Fort was thoroughly acquainted with them; his data give UFOs a history.

Pondering them all—fairy crosses and tiny coffins in Scotland, or brightly luminous balls bouncing about during earthquakes, or UFOs—one thinks again of Rudolf Steiner's quotation of Goethe's *Faust:* "Sink then! I might as well say, Mount! / 'Tis quite the same." We think of their extra-Sargasso Sea source as "up there," but one can as rightly think of them as coming from "down there"—from the Fire Earth. Ultimately as products of the etheric realm, they are directionless, precipitated from out of the cosmic, invisible, but eternally present, periphery. And many of them—especially those with the sulphurous smell, the injurious effect, the catastrophic consequence—are quintessentially Mephistophelean murmurings. Though Ahriman may be chained by Christ in the earth's interior, he has another province (called by esotericists the "Eighth Sphere") where his minions increasingly manifest their mischief. On the very rare occasions when Rudolf Steiner spoke of the Eighth Sphere, he did so with noticeable caution and circumspection. Identifying it as a supersensible realm between the Earth and the Moon, that is closely linked to the forces of the Fire Earth, Steiner hinted that this sphere was growing and strengthening due to the materialist thought life of modern men.

One wonders what was the nature of the conversation between Governor Woodbury and Bishop Michaud on that July day in 1907, whether the men argued over some fine point of theological doctrine, or politics. There must have been a good deal of passion to have called up that cigar-shaped exploding fireball and the ensuing cloudburst! Perhaps the two men even entertained the possibility that their own inner state had conjured the outer "sign." This was still a moment when, within the realm of academic psychology, one could consider the question of mind's relationship with matter. In March 1909, on Carl Jung's second visit with Sigmund Freud, after Jung told the skeptical Freud about certain paranormal experiences he had had, and Freud replied "Bosh!", Jung felt heat rise up in his solar plexus, just before a sound like a gunshot rang out from the bookcase. Jung explained that this was a "catalytic exteriorization phenomenon"—*aka* poltergeists—which Freud again dismissed. And again the shot rang out.

Poltergeists had a long history in America before July 2, 1907; earthquakes had a long history before December 28, 1908; magnetic storms had a long history before September 25, 1909. But round about this time, something was newly afoot in the Earth's ether, as if Christ's approach had stirred His cosmic adversary Ahriman. Steiner taught that electricity and electromagnetism were sub-earthly forces, and posed a challenge for humanity. The only challenge that Marconi, Edison, or the Edison Electric Light & Power Company could foresee was how to bring these new forces completely under control, and then bring them to as many parts of the globe as possible. At the advent of the Electric Age, say, on that September night in New York Harbor, how did it feel to the beings of the etheric world when the dark night exploded from the barrage of incandescent, arc, and searchlights equal to 26 million candles? Could the solar flares that ignited the auroral storm upon the Earth have been a *response* to the shock of human beings so decisively destroying the sanctity of the night?

In his January 1, 1909 lecture, Steiner had quoted another phrase from Goethe's *Faust*—"The little folk never scent the Devil / Even though he have them by the collar"—and stressed that those who claimed to be above medieval superstition would do well to remember those words. Charles Fort came very close to suggesting the same. Part Two of Goethe's *Faust*—almost a primer on the sub-earthly domain of Ahriman—was well-known to the Commissioners of the Champlain and Hudson-Fulton celebrations, all of whom were college-educated, progressive men. Faustian as their actions and ambitions were, they never seemed aware of how seductively Mephistopheles was whispering in their ear. Indeed, the distinct absence of the Devil from all of the commemorations' cultural activities only reinforced the truth of Goethe's maxim.

Anyone searching for Mephistopheles in Burlington in 1909 would not have had to look farther than the classrooms at the University of Vermont (UVM). The most popular student notebooks of the day were "Electric" notebooks. The cover illustration showed a pretty young woman telegraph operator, and behind her, in a sort of dream image, were electric poles and lines, leading to a brightly lit street lamp, from which emanated the word "E-L-E-C-T-R-I-C-I-T-Y." While their parents had been devotées of Spiritualism, mesmerism, animal magnetism, and phrenology, the typical American college student in 1909 was instead spellbound by the wonders of electricity. Electricity was modern *manitou*, some essence that could not be seen, smelled, or touched, and yet miraculously animated things.

But a more spectacular glimpse into how banal Mephistopheles had become to this first twentieth century American generation could be seen at the local Burlington ritual called "Kakewalk." In the winter of 1893, cabin-fever afflicted students from UVM fraternities had staged "an impromptu stag masquerade" complete with "cavaliers, coons, Indians, and imps" in the loft above the chapel in Old Mill, the main campus building. The students modeled their masque on the festivals and extravaganzas that had grown up in America alongside the centennial celebrations and world's fairs. Many of the students had recently visited the World's Columbian Exposition at Chicago, and taken away vivid memories of the Midway Plaisance, where alongside dancing, drumming and singing Dahomean villagers they'd seen black and white entertainers in blackface makeup performing the latest "coon songs." The hottest tunes were "cakewalks," dance tunes akin to two-steps or marches, that had been taken from African-American folk culture and were being turned out by the dozens mostly by white tunesmiths. In the 1890s, cakewalks were a national (and international) dance craze, no doubt a relief to piano-studying schoolboys and girls drilled in mechanical Czerny exercises and dusty old parlor tunes. They were also surely a relief from waltzes and quadrilles, and the 1893 UVM masquerade ended with a wild cakewalk dance competition, with costumed couples vying for the prize cake. Music was provided by three fiddles, a melodeon, and trombone, and after the competition, a keg of beer was opened up and everyone danced. The fiddlers worked the dancers into such a frenzy that they demolished the prize cake and knocked over the keg. When University faculty discovered puddles of beer in the chapel on Monday, "Kake Walk" was banned from campus.

By 1895, the event was a red letter day in the academic calendar, and the "Kulled Koons' Kakewalk" took place in the Old State Armory, where fraternity brothers teamed up to do the cakewalk in pairs, competing against one another for a prize cup. In 1896 classes were even dismissed for the day. In 1901, a parade was added, and two years later the event had moved to the new university gymnasium, to hold the ever-increasing crowd. Organizers moved the date to the weekend of Washington's Birthday, conjoining their local celebration with the national holiday. Within a decade having become Burlington's most elaborate public event, Kakewalk was anxiously anticipated for months, coming like carnival just as winter's frozen darkness had become too much to bear.

Before the cakewalk competition, fraternities put on skits that used vaudeville slapstick to poke fun at professors, local politicians, and themselves. Though women had been at UVM since 1872, all the actors were male, many of them performing in drag, and they parodied female basketball teams, temperance activists, and suffragettes. In these early years of Kakewalk, the most successful skits were those that employed the most elaborate "electrical" effects, such as this one, by Alpha Zeta, in 1912:

A gong struck! Through the utter blackness of the hall appeared miscellaneous arms, legs, a head and dismembered bodies of a phosphorescent character, all of which kept disappearing and appearing here and there in remote parts of the hall. Suddenly a comet with a fiery tail shot through the air. Instantly all the dissected bodies vanished and in the middle of the hall there arose a huge, glowing devil with weird, fantastic steps and then gradually faded away into invisibility. The lights flashed on. Not a sign of apparatus or of human life was to be seen on the floor!

In 1909, skits included "The Gleeful, Gruesome Ghouls," in which Sigma Nu brothers dressed up as medical students attempted to rob a grave along with their professor, only to be put to flight by the sudden appearance of the "Powers of the Night"—a troop of devils, headed by a diabolical fiddler. The same evening saw "The Infernal Question: Presented by His Satanic Majesty and Followers." In 1910, Alpha Tau Omega presented "His Majesty's Game;" an old miser counting his gold was surprised by the Devil, who turned the gold into death's heads, which promptly gave the miser a heart attack. A reviewer commented that the acting in this skit was excellent, "but unfortunately the electrical effects failed to come off as scheduled." That same evening, the audience was treated to Sigma Phi's "The Mystical Incubation," in which a farmer went to sleep over his poultry records and dreamed of a giant hen laying gargantuan eggs. A "master-devil" hatched her eggs, and each time he touched them with his pitchfork a red or green devil leapt from the eggs in a burst of flame. While the hatched devils danced to two violins, the master-devil magically flew off. There followed "Robert Houdin in the King's Garden," which again used lighting and sound effects to augment the magician's tricks, and then Sigma Nu staged "An Indian Pow Wow, or Willie Went West." Willie fell in with some "red-men" ("The make-ups were very good," said the review in the *University Cynic*) who scalped him and then burned him at the stake.

The appearance of Indians amidst the minstrelsy and devilry was not at all surprising. The first Kakewalk had seen a "Pea Souper" (French-Canadian) and a "Tommy" (Irishman) dancing with black women, but the masquerade quickly encompassed Cubans, Phillipinos, Puerto Ricans, Japanese, Indians, and of course, Africans and

African-Americans. From "Rain-in-the-Face" and "Butting Sill," from "Nigger Babies" and "Liliuokalami, the Chemical Queen of the Sandwich Islands," to local yokels (like "Reuben Haystack and Family" and "Two Rubes from Monkton"), Kakewalk took aim at all who were not white, male, and middle-class: the diabolical, done up in red crepe and domesticated by the buffoonery of the fraternity skits; the devouring female, in drag, the butt of one-liners familiar to the entire audience; America's most significant Other—the black man—in the guise of the happy-go-lucky dancing slave; and the Indian, America's other Other, too potent to be so humiliatingly emasculated.

The other big event of the academic year was the Peerade, which had likely been inspired by the circus parades that visited Burlington each summer. In the Peerade, the little boys who had thrilled to watch the circus come to town got a chance to become "carnies" for a day. The big parade departed from campus behind UVM President Matthew Buckham, a couple of UVM deans, Mayor John Burke, and other local celebrities, marching down Pearl Street to the tune of the college band. There followed "Curiosities and monstrosities from every continent, floats, barges and automobiles with wonderful cargoes." Most colorful were the various primitives that students had met in Professor George Perkins' anthropology class. There were Turks, Arabs, Indians, Zulus, Irish, Dutch, and Hebrew, along with civilized primitives—suffragettes, brides-and-grooms, babies and their nurses, hoboes, rubes, barkers, and clowns. Of the annually shifting groups of "wild men," two categories were always present—Indians and Zulus. The parade African was similar to his image in the skits, where he was alternately threatening and docile. The African cooking pot, tended by menacing "Zulu warriors," was a standard Kakewalk motif and cliché. But the Zulu could be tamed: in 1910, a local businessman presented two students with the trophy for best Kakewalk costume for their pantomime of a white hunter leading by means of a nose ring a nearly-naked Zulu. In some skits, the equation of Africans with animals was overt, borrowing from the stereotypy of the carnival freak show. The students also drew upon the lessons of their other course with Professor Perkins. Beginning in 1890, all UVM freshmen were required to attend weekly lectures by Perkins on "hygiene," broaching such topics as masturbation (it would lead to feeblemindedness), intercourse (a necessary evil), and an incipient sort of race hygiene in its portrayal of the non-white and lower class as dirty and potentially polluting.

Sometimes all these elements—the magical, the demonic, the primitive—melded together into a single skit, such as 1908's "Sure-paw and Fells Brothers, Grand Annex and Museé, Freaks, Curiosities, Monstrosities." In this one performance a group of students laid bare their era's vision of humanity. Along with the magical wizards—"Signor Zoroaster, the Strongest Man on Earth," "Mlle. Zendervesta, the Snake Charmer" and "Madame Rosalie La Grange, Mindreader and Thaumaturgist"—the skit had "Hee-Shee the Monkey Girl of the Yucatan" and "Jo-Jo the Philippine Leopard Boy." In their original venues, sandwiched between blackface minstrel shows, troupes of "Hawaiian" dancers, wild men of Borneo, gypsies, prodigies, "Aztecs," and other "curiosities," these freaks were presented in mock-scientific fashion, as "missing links." At the Kakewalk, racism was good, clean fun.

UVM's mid-winter masquerade was a grand unveiling of the mythological heart of middle class New England circa 1900. The parade of sorcerers, demons, and wild men, red and black, was a much more telling pageant than the Champlain Tercentenary's, for these caricatures spoke plainly of those elements which caused this community the greatest anxiety. An editorial in the student newspaper in the early 1900s declared about Kakewalk: "All this expense, and time, and labour, may not contribute greatly to the accumulated wisdom of the world, but it helps to knit together, in a centre of common interest, the various student groups." What truly knit together the students, faculty, and Burlington community was their entanglement in a mental fabric that conflated slaves, women, Indians, magicians, and devils.

"His Satanic Majesty," though never discussed in the anthropology class, was the most visible figure at Kakewalk, and the key to unraveling the psychic warp of this ritual celebration. Usually played by one of UVM's most histrionic devils, Mephistopheles presided over the very first Kakewalk celebrations, and if you flip through UVM yearbooks from around 1890 to 1910, you find that

Satan and his underlings stare back from many of the pages. The earliest illustrations for Kakewalk feature devils, sometimes presiding over boiling cauldrons in which sit clean-cut college boys. In the 1893 yearbook, the "Fraternities" section is illustrated by a black widow spider at the center of a web strewn with insects that have student's heads. The spider's face is a death's head. In 1894, a bucking bull is depicted tethered outside a row of stables, each stall topped by Greek letters. The following year shows a skull-shaped rock arch, with a crypt surmounted by a skull dimly visible at the center. In other years, skeletons and devils were joined by bats, snakes, monsters, and black cats.

The title page of the "Fraternities" section of the 1896 yearbook has a shrouded skeleton running along with a torch, accompanied by a charging black bull. The skeleton looks back, past its gloved left hand, whose middle finger is defiantly raised. Turning the page, one finds the devils' dens. Each of the fraternity insignias have one or more of these elements in them—death's head, skull and crossbones, devils, snakes, fire. Just as dreams took the "civilized" into the phenomenological realm of the "primitive," the gods of those fetishistic peoples had become the demons of the white men who had conquered and then begun to study them. Kakewalk stunts took the symbols of the old gods and lampooned them so irreverently that the symbols could no longer effectively communicate how frightening they had once been—or how real they might still be. It was the innocence of instinct that the masquerading students seemed to yearn for. In blackface or redface they could slip back into a body, dance and sing in a spontaneity denied them in their whiteness. Out on the dancing ground of carnival, the detested aboriginals gave back life to their white oppressors.

Kakewalk's Mephistopheles seemed to be trying to give something back. The students had originally resurrected the satanic to make a mockery of the community's Puritanism, but Puritanism prevailed, as the carnival was quickly made routine. Instead of digesting the repressive structures of the university, the community, and of winter's hold on mind and body, Kakewalk became one more structure of repression, quickly devolving into competitive athleticism in the University gymnasium and theater and into degenerate Bacchanalian orgy in the streets outside. Soon the hallmarks of the event were the drunkenness and trophies. Still, every year the refrain was heard —"This year Kakewalk is bigger and better than ever." This was the promise of the swarm, of the crowd, the promise of perpetual increase. But instead of dancing and parading to a place where they might meet and embrace their masqueraded aboriginal counterparts, the Kakewalk celebrants marched to a Dance of Death that required an ever-higher pile of skulls.

4

UNDER THE SIGN OF MARS

IN AN AGE OF RAPID CHANGE, anniversaries promise stability and continuity, and no age and place seized on anniversaries as tenaciously as America at the turn of the twentieth century. The Champlain and Hudson-Fulton organizers felt it was important to provide a wide public with mementos of these anniversaries. One of the first actions of the Hudson-Fulton Commission was to design an official seal: in the foreground, the "genius of the Hudson River"—a buxom, classically-garbed goddess—stood on the prow of a ship, the river and the Palisades behind her. In her right hand she held a shield bearing the inscription "Henry Hudson, 1609," in her left "Robert Fulton, 1807." There was also an official medal minted by the American Numismatic Society, showing on the face Henry Hudson standing on the deck of the *Half Moon*. On the rear, seated in front of a pair of Greek columns, were pictured the goddesses of: Commerce (resting her right hand on an anchor); History (a pen in her hand and scroll across her lap); and between them, the Goddess of Steam Navigation, holding a replica of the *Clermont* in her lap. The Final Report of the Hudson-Fulton Commission included a seven-page section describing the Official Medal, stressing its craftsmanship and historical accuracy. The artist consulted eminent astronomers, examined collections of historic navigational instruments, and made several visits to Holland to get input on his representation of Hudson's ship and the uniforms of his sailors. The spelling of names as they were written in 1609 required extensive research, as did the details of the *Clermont's* construction. After finding that no authentic portrait of Hudson existed, he was pictured in vague—but heroic—profile.

Four-inch diameter medals in solid silver were presented to the Commissioners and important guests; three-inch gold medals (executed by Tiffany & Company) to heads of nations; 2½ "bronze medals to participants in the official banquet and the aquatic games; two-inch aluminum medals for public sale; and 1½ "pocket pieces— at a dime apiece—for "visiting sailors."

There were in addition an Official Badge—bearing the image of the white-robed, angel wing-helmeted "Spirit of Progress" holding replicas of the *Half Moon* and the *Clermont*; Official Flag—between four and five million were sold during the Celebration; Official Poster—53,000 were given to railroad companies; Official Programs & Souvenirs—including 64—page brochures illustrating both the Historical and Carnival Parade Floats; and 72 different souvenir postcards. There was also a commemorative postage stamp issued on the opening day of the Celebration.

While there was as with Hudson no authentic portrait of Samuel de Champlain, the Tercentenary Commissioners made do with a painting of Louis XIV's Minister of Finance—one that had been used for over a century as Champlain's own likeness. Along with adorning the Official Invitation, Seal, Badge, and other souvenir items, the Finance Minister's face was immortalized in two life-sized bronze statues, one at Plattsburgh and the other at the Champlain Memorial Lighthouse at Crown Point. All of these talismans large and small bore upon them the dates "1609" and "1909," magically tying the two historical moments together forever.

Two other anniversaries were making headlines in 1909: the opposition of the earth with Mars (though Mars oppositions happen about every 26 months, every 15 or 17 years, opposition occurs within a few weeks of Mars' perihelion—the point in its orbit when it is closest to the sun—and the last time this had happened had been in 1894) and the return—after 76 years—of Halley's Comet. Beginning in the spring of 1909, American newspapers had been filled with talk about Mars's approach, largely inspired by the speculation of astronomer Percival Lowell, who had interpreted Italian astronomer Giovanni Schiaparelli's observations of *canali* (lines) on the red planet as "canals"—and thus as evidence of an advanced civilization. With books like *Mars as the Abode of Life* (1908), Lowell had popularized the idea that the planet was inhabited, and Americans in 1909 were caught up in the exciting prospect that its close approach might provide a definitive answer to the question of a Martian civilization. Harvard astronomer William Henry Pickering proposed communicating with Mars via a $10 million array of mirrors, and while the international astronomical community ridiculed his idea, French astronomer Camille Flammarion thought it likely that the Martians—living on a planet older than the Earth, and thus "infinitely superior intellectually to us"—were *already* signaling the Earth.

Electrical wizard Nikola Tesla agreed, claiming that in the summer of 1899 he had detected electrical disturbances—i.e., signals—from Mars. Tesla called for a quarter-million square foot reflector if the mirror plan were to be put into effect, but suggested that his own wireless transmitter would be the best method. A *Times* editorial compared Flammarion's image of Martians—"light blue in color, amiable in disposition, somewhat like human beings, but not nearly so gross—winged, buoyant, and charming"—with that of H.G. Wells, who saw them with brains so powerful that their arms and legs had long ago disappeared from disuse, so that they now appeared as "huge, unlovely oysters with innumerable tentacles of great power." The *Times* editor dismissed both views, musing instead upon the fact that the Martians must "wonder why we have nothing to say for ourselves." Another *Times* writer penned an imagination of a future 2009 commemoration, in which the opening day highlight would be a rendezvous over the Hudson of "Earthian" spaceships with those of other planets. Friday there would be round trip flights to Mars for spectators—at $17 a ticket.

Just as 1909 was the first hundred-year anniversary of Champlain and Hudson's expeditions since the invention of telegraphy, automobiles, and airships, 1910's return of Halley's Comet was the first since the invention of photography, and it was widely anticipated that revealing pictures would be captured of the cometary visitor. The comet would not reach its closest approach to Earth until the spring of 1910, but the first sighting occurred (in Heidelberg, Germany) on September 11, 1909, and this set off a flurry of interest among both press and public. Professor William Hallock of Columbia University gave instruction about the comet in a full-page *New York Times* spread. The article featured a large drawing of a passenger ship on the Hudson River with the Manhattan skyline behind, in the sky above it a map of the course of the comet from its first sighting on September 11th through the constellation Taurus, then past the Pleiades. Hallock detailed Edmond Halley's observations of the comet, stressing his breakthrough discovery of its 76-year periodicity. Astronomers reassured anxieties that in passing through the comet's tail, Earth would not be enveloped by deadly cyanide gas. It would, one scientist said, be like "a gentle breeze distribut[ing] the smoke of a campfire over a good-sized country." But by 1910 there were opportunists hawking "Comet Pills" to protect the gullible from Halley's expected dreadful effects.

Though scientists had only in 1909 discovered by spectrographic analysis that comets contain cyanide, Rudolf Steiner had revealed this in a lecture in Paris in 1906. Here his clairvoyance and natural science agreed, but as to the actual nature of comets Steiner's views diverged greatly from the physicists and astronomers. Speaking about Halley's Comet in 1910, Steiner said that it influences the human Ego so that it becomes more closely attached to the physical body—especially the brain. A necessary, beneficial task in the history of mankind, ensuring that the Ego stayed connected to the physical realm of Earth, Steiner warned that Halley's Comet, if not met with in the right way in 1910, would acquire a dangerous materialistic character.

Steiner emphasized that Halley's Comet was a cosmic phenomenon inextricably linked to the reappearance of Christ in the etheric, presenting humanity with a great challenge:

> In the present year 1910 we are experiencing a new appearance of the ancient comet, and that signifies a year of crisis. . . . All the forces are at work there to give birth to a still shallower and worse sense in the human soul, to create a materialistic 'bog.' Man is placed before a mighty test, a trial to determine whether, alongside the threat of deepest descent, the impulse to ascend can prevail. For otherwise it would not be possible for man to overcome the resistance which the materialistic

view puts in his way. If man were not exposed to materialism, he would not be able to overcome it out of his own forces. And now the opportunity is offered him to choose between the spiritual and the materialistic path. The terms for this year of crisis are sent us from the cosmos.

Steiner recalled the year 1872, when, as a boy living with his parents in a small railroad station (where his father was a telegraph operator!) on the Puszta plain near the border of what is today Croatia and Hungary, there was widespread fear that the world was about to be destroyed by Biela's Comet, which had appeared in 1845/6 and again in 1852. By that time, the comet had split in two, and when it reappeared in 1872, it did so as a brilliant November meteor shower rather than as a threat to planet Earth. Indeed, asserted Steiner, Biela's Comet and *all* comets contributed to the Earth minute amounts of cyanide, which was taken up by plants and eventually ingested by human beings, whose astral bodies were purified by the tiny dose of poison.

There was no individual on the planet as cheered by comets as Rudolf Steiner, who called them the "freedom-heroes of the cosmos":

> There is an immensely great cosmic physician at work in the cosmos who is more or less constantly busy administering therapies like this. Just think: What we see above us as a comet in the sky in one period then becomes atomized as I have described; it comes down from the sky in showers of fire; later it is in the soil and still later it moves from the soil into the plants, into their roots, stems, leaves and flowers. We eat the cometary deposit, the cometary leaven that is given to the earth by the cosmos, we eat it with our very bread.

As he said about Halley's Comet, comets *could* become harbingers of disaster, but only if humanity remained asleep, under the spell of materialism that Halley's Comet had once rightfully come to foster. Then, remarkably, Rudolf Steiner pointed to the same year as he had when he announced the advent of the Etheric Christ:

> My dear friends, in 1933 there would have been the possibility that the earth, with all that lives on it, could have been wiped

out if another, wise and incalculable influence were not to come into effect—for calculations cannot always be right when comets assume their other form.

Just as the German astronomer Littrow in 1832 had calculated that Biela's Comet would strike the earth in 1872, but it had not done so due to its breaking up, Steiner seemed to suggest that this same comet would have collided with the earth in 1933, but for "wise and incalculable influences."

Saying that "Satan lies in wait for every comet that turns up," Steiner asserted that Satan and his "mighty cohorts" act to divert the movement of comets to disrupt the earth's and other planets' orbits, but that the Archangel Michael works to keep this from happening. Still, having forestalled the disaster from without, the spiritual world permitted another one to unfold from within, *beginning in 1933*. In identifying the year 1933, Steiner spoke of a different adversary of Christ than Ahriman:

> At the end of the century we come to a time when Sorath again raises his head most powerfully from the surrounding flood of evolution. He will oppose the vision of Christ which will appear in the etheric world to those who are prepared to receive it in the first half of the twentieth century. . . .

Steiner spoke publicly about Sorath only six other times in his life. The first occasion was on April 22, 1907, when he discussed Chapter 13 of John's *Apocalypse*, where John says that the number of the Beast is 666. Steiner explained that the numbers should be read as the Hebrew letters *Samech* (60); *Vau* (6); *Resh* (200); and *Tau* (400), giving the name *Sorath* and the number 666. He translated Sorath to mean "Demon of the Sun," explaining that every star had both its good spirit and its demon, and thus Sorath was the adversary of Christ.

The second time Steiner spoke about the Sun Demon was over a year later, on June 29, 1908—less than 12 hours before the catastrophic explosion above the Tunguska River fir forest in Siberia. Clearly, if one looks at Rudolf Steiner's perennial ability to be in the right place at the right time, this July 29 lecture suggests that he anticipated some impending activity of the Sun Demon. That scientists continue to be completely mystified by the Tunguska event is compelling evidence for the limits of materialist science, which would also miss the significance of the *place* of Steiner's 1908 lecture—in Nuremberg, where, Steiner clearly intuited, the Beast would at a future date rise from the abyss, just as John's *Apocalypse* had declared nearly two thousand years ago.

In 1909, Americans were less wary than Europeans of German militarism, and so at the Hudson-Fulton celebration—where German warships joined the Naval Parade, and the German delegation was headed by Grosadmiral Hans von Koester—Germany was a welcome guest. One of the most fundamental reasons for the success of both the Champlain and Hudson-Fulton celebrations was that America was at peace in 1909, and naively looked forward to a twentieth century of peace as well as progress. The Sun Demon had other plans, and Rudolf Steiner may have been the only human being on the planet who foresaw those plans. On October 13, 1918, the very same night that Corporal Adolf Hitler lost consciousness in a trench on the frontline at Ypres after a British mustard gas attack, Steiner again spoke of the Beast, by way of speaking of the Academy of Gondhishapur in Persia around the year AD 666. In the wake of the Byzantine Emperor Justinian's closing of the great philosophical schools, teachers fled to this academy, where they fell under the influence of its master, an unnamed individual who "was the greatest opponent of Christ Jesus." In identifying this seventh century individual who provided a vessel for Sorath to inhabit, Steiner was bearing silent witness to the Sun Demon's return to the physical plane, at the very moment that the Beast took hold of the diminished consciousness of Adolf Hitler.

When, on the first day of 1909, Steiner had responded to the audience member's question about whether an initiate could foresee earthquakes and other catastrophes, and then warn of them, he had said that "it is actually only twice or three times in any one century—at the very most, twice or three times—that any prediction can be announced from the centers of Initiation." This esoteric rule was predicated on the need to leave humanity free to reckon with its own karma, and to develop on its own its capacity to recognize the significance of such events. At the heart of Steiner's spiritual practice was a new and courageous Manicheism that accepted evil as a challenge to be overcome and transformed for the achievement of higher levels of spiritual evolution. Steiner's seemingly oblique ways of warning about the Beast—both in the case of the Tunguska event and Hitler's possession by Sorath—were careful and respectful attempts to encourage initiative on the part of his listeners. One cannot know exactly what Steiner's inner vision saw that night as he was lecturing in Nuremberg, but his clairvoyance surely took in more than just the moment of Hitler's possession, perhaps extending forward to the Nazi party rallies of 1933 to 1938, when the Sun Demon held forth before hundreds of thousands of mesmerized Germans.

Steiner stressed always that both Sorath and Ahriman are totally dependent upon *not* being recognized by humanity. One can search the thousands of books written about Hitler, and not a single one will so much as hint in the direction of demonic possession. Ian Kershaw's recent massive two-volume biography of Hitler passes over the mustard gas attack episode in a single page, drawing no conclusion at all from the radical transformation of personality that ensued immediately after Hitler regained consciousness. One need only listen to Hitler's words to hear the Sun Demon proclaiming his desire to put himself in the place of the Sun Spirit. "The work begun by Christ, I will bring to a conclusion!" Hitler declared at a Christmas celebration in 1926. In 1933, a week and a half after seizing power, he parodied the Lord's Prayer when he promised that under him a new kingdom would come on earth, and that this would be "the power and the glory, Amen." Hitler referred to "the holy year of our Lord 1933"—which included January 30, the day Hitler seized power, as a Nazi holiday—and made his own birthday the day when Hitler Youth were "baptized" in their faith. "You are flesh of our flesh and blood of our blood" he told the Hitler Youth at a 1934 rally, and in 1932 advised them either to be "hot or cold, but lukewarm should be damned and spewed from your mouth."

Revelations 3:15–16 reads: "I know thy words. Thou art neither cold nor hot; I would thou wert cold or hot. So then because thou art lukewarm, and neither cold nor hot, I will spew thee out of my mouth." But neither Germany nor the world recognized Hitler's words as the voice of the Beast. In Goethe's *Faust*, after Mephistopheles succeeded in getting Faust to sign the pact in blood, he shouted his triumph:

> Reason and knowledge only thou despise
> The highest strength in man that lies!
> Let but the Lying Spirit bind thee
> And I shall have thee fast and sure!

When human thinking ceases, both Steiner and Goethe taught, a door is opened for Sorath to enter, and in the case of Hitler and the German people, Sorath's binding spell was well nigh complete. Augmenting his words with hypnotizing gestures, Hitler executed the most demonic form of black magic, while the Beast hid in plain sight before the entire world.

The Sun Demon, Steiner taught, is incapable of any creative power, and thus must always "borrow"—down to the smallest detail—the forms of the Divine. The path of the Sun Spirit Christ—especially in the twentieth century, when humanity was fully individualized in the Ego—was the path of the spiritualization of thinking; the enkindling of feeling; and the illumination of the will by becoming conscious of one's higher destiny. In place of this path, Hitler/Sorath led Germany and the world down a path that paralyzed the thinking; killed compassion and conscience; and brutalized the will, ending in fanaticism. Hitler reversed Christ's maxim "Thy will be done" to "*My* will be done," and a nation submitted.

BURLINGTON

From the summer of 1909 until 1929, on the wall of the apartment he called "Bachelorest" at the corner of Maple and South Union Street, Byron N. Clark proudly displayed his official invitation from the Governor of New York and the Tercentenary Commission to the "Three Hundredth Anniversary of the Discovery of Lake Champlain." The invitation bore the Official Seal: four medallions with images of: the faux Champlain; "Magua"—an Iroquois chief wearing a Plains Indian headdress; and the ruins of Fort Ticonderoga and

Fort Frederick. Above the medallions hovered the Great Seal of the United States, and behind them were arranged a branch of white oak leaves; a white pine bough; musket; a bow and a quiver of arrows; a tomahawk and sword. Though both seals were supposed to symbolize the power of war and peace together, the olive, pine, and oak branches were overshadowed by all the images of war, from the weapons to the stone ruins of the colonial era forts. Byron Clark's life had been as conspicuously empty of martial vigor as his imagination was full of it. After high school he had worked as a printer, and the printing job that brought him to Burlington was turning out advertisements for Paine's Celery Compound, one of the many patent medicine tonics being sold to American men and women to combat their "exhaustion" from modern life. His apartment was filled with symbols of the strenuous life—a collection of colonial period firearms, snowshoes, moccasins, a walking stick, an ash pack basket, deer antlers, and Navajo rugs. Small statuettes of perfect Greek physiques decorated the mantel. Settled in among all this clutter and his sizable library was Clark, hardly resembling his Greek or frontier heroes. His typical attire was the stiff, heavily starched uniform of the middle class, and even out at Camp Abnaki—the YMCA boys' camp he had founded in 1901—he presented a rather unheroic figure, bespectacled, pudgy, always frowning, polo shirt buttoned tight at the neck, his collar up, making him look like a prudish, disapproving cleric. But he hoped to look at least part warrior, always wearing a knife and scabbard on his bulging belt.

There had been a strong martial strain at Camp Abnaki since its first summer at Cedar Beach, and with the rise in American militarism that accompanied World War I, Camp Abnaki, like most YMCA and Boy Scout summer camps across the country, emulated the adult world. In 1915 Theodore Roosevelt—an original member of the Boy Scout National Council—threatened to resign if BSA leaders who espoused pacifism were not removed. Roosevelt maintained that a Boy Scout who was not trained actively to bear arms was a "sissy." By 1917, boys at Camp Abnaki drilled once a day with wooden toy rifles, and a firing range was created so they could gain experience with real weapons. Camp Abnaki visitors, both in and out of military uniform, delivered plenty of martial rhetoric for the campers. Captain Charles A. Palmer of the Fourth Division of the Corps of Guides, Canada, had this advice for the Camp Abnaki boys: "We pray for Universal Peace and brotherhood, but for years to come there is but one motto, and that is: Trust in God and keep your rifle loaded." Francis Parkman's prescription—"to realize a certain ideal of manhood—a little medieval"—was one to which Byron Clark had long aspired, and the war in Europe added a touch of risk and danger to all the play-acting and storytelling about martial heroism at the camp.

Clark, who claimed that his own ancestry ran back to a nobleman who had served with William the Conqueror, was too old himself for active military service, and so he volunteered for overseas YMCA work. In September of 1917 he sailed to Europe aboard *La Touraine* with University of Vermont President Guy Potter Benton and other YMCA officials. Benton's European destination was Paris, where he assumed the office of General Secretary for the YMCA, while Clark headed for the Y camp in Bron, in the Rhone Valley, where the largest American air base was located. At the end of 1918, Clark was appointed "Sight-seeing Secretary," a position that gave him a very mild experience of the war. An avid photographer, Clark documented his sightseeing with pictures of groups of YMCA officials at meetings in Paris, their waiter on board *La Touraine*, Rheims Cathedral, the palace and casinos in Monaco, the Mediterranean coast at Nice. He had photos of heroic young aviators taking off on bombing runs, of Alsatian villagers, and mythic localities such as the camping place of Julius Caesar near Chateauvillain. But the only photos in his European album that showed the true carnage of the war were snapshots that he purchased, since he was far from the front lines. On page after page, he pasted in photos of French soldiers in trenches, of artillery and airplanes, bombed buildings and cemeteries filled with war victims. Occasionally he would add his own captions, such as the one penned in on the margin of a grisly scene of a corpse-filled trench at Verdun—"The price of glory!"

Since the Puritan-Indian wars, good Christian Americans like Clark had sought personal renewal through violent confrontation, and violence was a staple of the Camp Abnaki diet, along with the pork and potatoes served up by Mr. Lapier, the French-Canadian camp cook. Boxing, wrestling, and tug-of-war were all ritualized, safe forms that readily yielded to the true, authentic violence of war. Much of the impetus for the sort of character building practiced by Clark and other YMCA and BSA leaders was the fear among middle-class Americans that they were becoming enfeebled by modernity, and strenuous physical activity, even when it had no practical consequence or when the principal consequence was death and destruction, was seen as an antidote to enfeeblement. Clark had been a crusader for years, as a Sunday school teacher, and as a member of the Vermont Anti-Saloon League, the Masons, and various YMCA reforms, but all of these moral wars only heightened his desire for *authentic* experience. He fully shared his generation's fascination with all forms of disciplined vitality. In the Abnaki camp handbook, Clark spelled out the ethos:

> The sense of mastery, of victory in what we undertake, is a perpetual uplift to the life. It is a powerful tonic to ambition, a perpetual stimulus to endeavor. . . . There is a sense of added power in every victory, a feeling of enlargement at the very thought of overcoming. A feeling of exaltation thrills the whole system when we have proved ourselves master of the situation. There is an exhilaration which accompanies the sense of victory that makes us long to undertake even harder things. . . .

Clark's choice of Cedar Beach on Lake Champlain as a camping spot was fortuitous, since it afforded the sort of natural amphitheater so effective for imparting a sense of history and tradition to the boys. Behind the cedar-fringed shoreline of Lake Champlain rose Mount Philo, and behind that, the Green Mountains, while to the west, beyond the lake, the Adirondacks presented their massive front. Clark—an avid antiquarian who was a member of the Society of Colonial Wars in the State of Vermont, a founder of the Vermont Antiquarian Society, and author of a roster of the Vermont veterans of the War of 1812—could stand on the beach and narrate the exploits of the Allen brothers and the Green Mountain Boys, Benedict Arnold, Lieutenant Thomas Macdonough, and a host of other local war heroes.

Two weeks after the end of the 1901 camp season, Clark met with the boys to show his photographs of the experience. There were shots of the three canvas tents with their campers posed outside, photos of horseshoe playing, pillow fights, of Mr. Lapier tending the stewpot and hauling firewood. There were pictures of William Van Patten's steam yacht, the "Isolde," which had carried the campers off to explore the area of Fort Cassin on Otter Creek. The boys could see themselves fishing, boxing, and swimming. The images brought back memories of their first day in camp when, as soon as they had erected their tents, a storm had rolled across the lake from the Adirondacks. "Dad" (the campers' name for Clark) had told the cooped-up and restless boys a ghost story, and after dinner, he led them in the Lord's Prayer. The next morning, services were followed by a baseball game, and after lunch there was time to go hunt arrowheads and "lucky stones" along the shore. Though there were no photos of it, the thing the boys remembered most was the campfire, and the Indian tales Dad Clark told there. Story after story was related each evening, and a secret society rite—initiation into some mysterious entity entitled the "Midnite Devils"—had firmly established itself before week's end.

In 1909, inspired by the Tercentenary celebrations, the camp adopted "Abnaki" as its name. Like Ernest Thompson Seton's "Woodcraft Indians," which Seton founded at his Connecticut estate the summer after Clark's first Cedar Beach camp, Camp Abnaki drew heavily on Indian motifs to build its own traditions. Boys often took Indian-sounding names at the initiation rites, and each summer there were some who rigged makeshift loincloths and painted themselves with charcoal, red ochre, and the blue clay that cropped out along the lakeshore, for mock battles on the beach near camp. Dad Clark's campfire stories were often retellings of Indian legends he knew from C.G. Leland's *Algonquin Legends of New England* or Bureau of American Ethnology bulletins. At each campsite, pot-hunting forays uncovered material proof of Indians, and the arrowheads and pottery shards gave the boys a direct route back in time. Most summers, University of Vermont Professor George Henry Perkins would give the boys a lecture on Vermont Indians, and there were other visitors interested in Indian lore, including

Dillon Wallace, the Labrador explorer, who in 1914 regaled the boys with stories of the northern wilds. He told them of the tragic death of his partner Leonidas Hubbard, and gave instruction in tracking, building traps, camp cooking, and making "squaw bread." The boys were thrilled to hear that Wallace encountered real "wild Indians" on his expedition.

Having attended the Tercentenary Indian pageant, the boys at Camp Abnaki created their own pageant in the summer of 1909. Instead of the Tercentenary's celebration of warring Indians and empires, the Camp Abnaki pageant tried to foster a smaller, more tangible aspiration—to "right action" among one's neighbors. The "Herald" narrator proclaimed at the beginning of the drama: "And so, indeed, it is our earnest hope, / That in these simple scenes we here portray, / Of fact and fancy in our pageantry, / You may awake and youthful be again, / In dwelling in the days long since gone by, / When men were made of stronger build than now, / When stirring scenes were acted, blood was shed. . . ." The YMCA cult of manliness was like the New England cult of the heroic past, harking always to a time when men were physical and moral giants. Both cults grew out of acute anxiety over the apparent degeneration of the present. Though men were stronger then, they were still "moved like pawns in battle for the soil," like the players in the pageants.

Like other character builders of his era, Clark had a system for engendering "manliness," mainly through exercise. Clark admired the Indian physique and his ideal at camp was to emulate the Indian regimen of "natural" exercise by way of hiking and camping, but this was rarely done. When they first arrived at camp, Clark took tape measure, spring dynamometer, and scale to the boys, measuring the girth of their heads, the size of their forearms, their lung capacity, the depth of their chests, and the length and breadth of every conceivable body part. Having a clear image of what the ideal physique was, he suggested the necessary exercises to build up or shrink down those parts found wanting. Clark delighted in those who developed their physiques, filling his photo albums with individual and group portraits of naked and semi-naked boys in muscle poses. Most boys at the camp led a fairly sedentary life, housed in big canvas tents on platforms arranged in a straight row in an open

field. Each morning they spilled out onto the drill ground for calis-
thenics, and there was baseball, boxing, swimming and canoeing for
those who enjoyed such activities, but all of the activities resembled
boot camp more than an Indian camp.

Those boys who didn't build their bodies were subject to ridicule,
not only because of their undesirable flab, but because overly studi-
ous or non-athletic boys were suspected to be guilty of the "solitary
vice" of masturbation. Such a disruption of the "spermatic economy," which held that conservation of semen guaranteed mental
and physical vigor, would supposedly lead to enfeeblement, and
ultimately, to insanity. Camp Abnaki was a place for the absorption
and cultivation of power, not for its squandering, and the Camp
Abnaki tribe was tutored in its culture's methods of augmenting
male potency. Clark and other YMCA leaders lectured the campers
each summer on hygiene, telling them that masturbation was not
only a sin, but that it led to dangerous depletion of the "nerve
force," since reabsorbed semen gave one strength.

Every 15 to 17 years, when Mars swung round to approach the
Earth, America looked up into the night sky with certain anticipa-
tions of outer danger, but with no sense that the red planet stirred
within them any dangerous inner propensities. The nation had long
ago forgotten that Mars's higher aspect was the cultivation of inner
moral courage—like that of Henry David Thoreau or Frederick
Douglass—and instead succumbed to the neighboring planet's
lower aspect of cruel and aggressive violence. That aspect found
muted expression everywhere during the 1909 commemorative
events, which were at their core celebrations of the triumph of civilized white men over red savages—a triumph at the moment being
replayed in the lingering violence of America's occupation of the
Philippines. On the second day of the Tercentenary, the *Burlington
Free Press* dispassionately reported recent developments there: "In a
desperate fight near Patan on Iolo Island yesterday the famous
Moro chief Jirikiri was killed and his entire band exterminated by
detachments of regulars and constabulary under George L. Byrem
of the Sixth U.S. Cavalry."

During his Tercentenary address in Burlington, former Secretary
of War and newly elected President William Howard Taft confessed

that he knew little about Champlain or the other French explorers, but said that in the Philippines, where he had served as Governor-General, he had encountered their same spirit in the Spanish explorers, "controlled men equally brave, and in certain respects more successful—Magellan, Legaspi. . . ." Taft used to love to go to the public square in Manila, where there was a statue of Legaspi holding the Spanish standard in one hand, a drawn sword in the other. Behind him was a Rigeletto monk holding a cross above his head. Even on hot days, Taft would go and stand in front of it, so that he might feel "such movement, such force, such courage."

Under Taft, America in the Philippines had wed the sword and the cross with genocidal effect. Taft, along with the American soldiers who attacked the Philippines, and the American people, were all completely at home calling the indigenous people there "Indians," and in this latest Indian War, the combination of fierce patriotism and Christian doctrine labeling non-Christians as morally inferior beings led to a decade of atrocities that hardly stirred the American conscience. When he appeared before Congress and casually mentioned the use of the "so-called water cure" to extract information from Philippine natives, Taft needed to make no apology, since most Americans saw the victims as less-than-human savages.

America's domestic Indian wars were not overlooked by the Tercentenary speakers. Before an audience at Crown Point, Seth Low lauded America's policy of moving to the west "tribes that had proved themselves to be uncomfortable neighbors in the eastern portion of the country," and he defended the confinement of Indians on reservations by saying that this practice protected them from "utter destruction" by civilization. The fantasy of Native American extinction seemed to be confirmed by current events. 1909 was the year that the J. P. Morgan-funded photo and textual documentation of North American Indians by Edward S. Curtis began to win wide public attention. In Curtis's multi-volume *The North American Indian*—the result of his photo-ethnography salvage tour of aboriginal America—the U. S. public was treated to a museum-view of the Noble Savage in brown and white. The ghostly auras that hung around his Indian subjects suggested not only nobility but evanescence, as if they might slip from view at any moment. Curtis's paid

Indian models were posed in only traditional-looking scenes, dressed in leather and feathers, with earth and sky as backdrop. The trappings of the present, the accommodations of the Indian to white culture—watches, clocks, suspenders—were carefully retouched or cropped to obliterate them from the photographs. And the twenty volumes of *The North American Indian* contained no images of eastern Indians, no Mohawk steelworkers, no Abenaki lumberjacks, no Algonquin hunting guides. Curtis' work "vanished" the Indian in its very celebration.

1909 was the year that the Apache chief Geronimo and Red Cloud, the Sioux leader, died, and the year that Chief Crazy Snake led an unsuccessful uprising of Creeks and Seminoles in Oklahoma. In South Dakota, the government was seeking to open ten million acres of reservation lands for settlement by white farmers; in Flathead and Coeur d'Alene country, another half-million acres was facing the same prospect. Thousands of Cherokees in Oklahoma were starving due to a drought. Newspaper front pages faithfully followed the California manhunt of the Paiute "murderer," Willie Boy. In December, the *New York Times* told its readers of the death of J. Harris, the famous rattlesnake-hunter guide, whom it reported was the last "full-blooded" Indian on the Schaghticoke reservation in Connecticut.

When Dad Clark and his boys—and thousands of other spectators—headed home from the Tercentenary pageant in Burlington carrying with them the memory of Iroquois and Algonquians in feathered war bonnets at the mock battle on the phony island, they had no sense that they were under the spell of the dark side of Mars. The twentieth century they would create showed the spell still held.

Zurich, Dornach, Stuttgart, 1919

The first Armistice Day, November 11, 1919, was meant to be a day of celebration of peace, and of commemoration of the millions of victims of World War I. More than four million Americans served during the war, and across America, there were hundreds of Armistice Day parades. In Centralia, Washington, as the memorial parade—

with its large contingent of American Legion members—passed in front of the Industrial Workers of the World Hall, a fight broke out. Legionnaire Post Commander Warren Grimm called out to halt the disturbance, and almost immediately was shot through the chest. Another Legionnaire standing near Grimm was killed by a bullet through the brain. As the men were dragged from the middle of the street, more shots rang out, and Legionnaires stormed the Wobbly Hall. As Wobbly Wesley Everest ran for the back of the hall, he shot and killed one Legionnaire and wounded another. Before he was captured, Everest killed one more and injured a second Legionnaire. As evening fell, a vigilante mob stormed the jail, abducted Everest, and hung him from a bridge.

The Centralia Massacre came in the wake of "Red Summer," when America saw race riots in Charleston, Washington, D.C., Chicago, Knoxville, Omaha, and more than a dozen other cities. Sparked by racism and unemployment, the riots were also fed by the growing Red Scare; anyone looking for better working conditions was branded a "Red," and subject to the sort of violence that had been principally reserved for blacks.

On November 11, 1919, Rudolf Steiner was in Dornach, Switzerland finishing a lecture series entitled "The Influences of Lucifer and Ahriman: Man's Responsibility for the Earth." In what was really the opening lecture of the series—"The Ahrimanic Deception"—given at the end of October in Zurich, Steiner had blamed the war on the "Ahrimanic powers," saying that they played upon nationalism and racism to set human beings against one another. While Steiner had spoken of Ahriman many times since that first day of 1909, when he linked the Messina earthquake to Ahriman, this occasion in 1919 was the first time that he ever spoke of an *incarnation* of Ahriman:

> Ahriman skillfully prepares his goal beforehand; ever since the Reformation and the Renaissance, the economist has been emerging in modern civilization as the representative governing type. That is an actual historical fact.... Rulers are in fact merely the handymen, the understrappers of the economists.... If men do not realize that the rights-state and the

organism of the Spirit must be set against the economic order called up through the economists and the banks, then again, through this lack of awareness, Ahriman will find an important instrument for preparing his incarnation. His incarnation is undoubtedly coming, and this lack of insight will enable him to prepare it triumphantly.

A couple of days later, in Dornach, Steiner narrowed the timeline for Ahriman's incarnation, saying it would come "before even a small part of the third millennium has run its course."

Many of his listeners had come to expect this sort of stunning statement, delivered calmly by "Herr Doktor." In a lecture series in December 1916, he spoke of a Russian government that was "to be swept away," and of secret Western brotherhoods that planned to "carry out certain quite definite economic experiments ... of a socialist nature." This was months before either the February Revolution or Lenin's October Revolution. A month later, in a series of lectures that diagnose the true causes of World War I, Steiner identified how these same secret societies had been responsible for starting World War I.

In Stuttgart just after Christmas in 1919, Steiner again revealed more about the impending incarnation of Ahriman when he made an almost offhand remark that Ahriman's name might be "John William Smith." With this, he clearly pointed to the incarnation taking place in the English-speaking West, but given other remarks about how strong the Ahrimanic forces were upon the North American continent, it is certain that he meant that the incarnation would take place in America.

There were only a handful of Americans who had joined the anthroposophical community at Dornach, and no doubt they were shocked at Steiner's prophecy. Given the heroism of the doughboys in the Great War, the Europeans too must have been shocked by such a pronouncement. Still, they knew Rudolf Steiner's maxim—that he never publicly spoke of any subject unless he had checked on its veracity thoroughly through his spiritual scientific research.

When he spoke of the incarnation of Ahriman or "Antichrist," Steiner frequently seemed to be describing not just one single individual, but a kind of social process in which many individuals would participate. In a reversal of the process that prepared the vessel—Jesus of Nazareth—for the incarnation of the Sun Spirit, the vessel for Antichrist would be created from the sum of the degenerate thoughts, feelings, and will of *all* human beings. Deadened materialistic thoughts would feed the fallen "Light Ether"—the same realm from which the force of electricity springs—and make possible the creation of an astral body for Ahriman. A lack of love for or interest in the spiritual world would intensify the "Chemical Ether" (the realm of magnetism), weaving an etheric body for Ahriman. Fear would paralyze human morality, contributing substance to the fallen "Life Ether," building an actual physical body for Ahriman. Once these three subtle bodies were completely built up, the Ego of Ahriman would be able to light up, in a demonic counter-image of Christ's incarnation into the bodies built up by Jesus of Nazareth.

Transcripts of Steiner's lectures on the incarnation of Ahriman indicate that his audience was too stunned to ask deeper questions about this frightening event. Even had the questions been asked, it seems that Rudolf Steiner would have answered in such a way as to leave a great deal of further research for subsequent generations to refine his indications, since this was a necessary part of the process of recognition that Steiner emphasized as a key to meeting this terrible encounter with Evil.

Just as in the incarnation of Christ, Ahriman would have assistance from both "above"—an even greater being than himself—and "below"—i.e., human assistance, more immediately and consciously than the assistance given by human beings' collective materialistic thoughts and deeds. Christ's deeds had all been performed in the open, on the physical plane; in fact, Christ's life at one level could be considered an enactment of all the ancient mysteries. Rudolf Steiner similarly threw wide the doors of the mysteries with the mystery school he founded when he began his work as an esoteric teacher in 1900, and which was formalized in 1913 with the creation of the Anthroposophical Society. There were, however, two other twentieth century mystery schools that possessed initiation knowledge—the Freemasons and the Jesuits. In the Jesuit initiation—founded by

Ignatius Loyola in 1540—intense exercises for training the will result in the candidate creating an occult bond with Lucifer rather than Christ. In the Freemasonic initiation—(Steiner typically referred to Masonry as "the Western lodges" or "Western brotherhoods")—rituals of ceremonial magic draw the candidate into a Faustian bond with Ahriman.

Rudolf Steiner pointed to a third stream of "counter-initiation" which had opened up in the twentieth century: "There are three streams of initiation involved here: two of them lie on the plane of human evolution [the Western lodges and the Jesuits] and then there is one with vast, almost immeasurably vast, strength of will forces which lie beneath it [Bolshevism]." Finally, in a less direct fashion, Steiner pointed to a fourth counter-initiation that was working in the world. In many instances, when Steiner said *nationalismus,* he was making a veiled reference to the particularly poisonous nationalism—Nazism—then arising from his own region. Rudolf Steiner characterized both Bolshevism ("The modern condition of Russia—this is what the demons of Sorath who are invading human souls are striving towards") and National Socialism ("Before the etheric Christ will be able to be rightly understood, mankind will have to cope with the Beast who will rise from the abyss in 1933") as movements inspired by and serving the goals of Sorath.

In *Occult Science: An Outline,* which he finished at the end of 1909, Steiner described an important law governing human spiritual evolution, which stated that every time evolution is about to rise to a new level, the previous stages are first recapitulated in a metamorphosed form. This law works for both the benevolent powers and the adversarial powers, again, due to the fact that evil cannot of itself act creatively in the universe.

When Steiner in 1909 unfolded Sorath's name in terms of the Kabbalistic number 666, he was also giving a key to the Sun Demon's rhythm in Time. The first occurrence of 666 after the Mystery of Golgotha had seen Sorath's attempt to foster at the Academy of Gondhishapur a premature and one-sided impulse that would influence the birth of modern science. The second occurrence, and thus the second historical manifestation of Sorath's influence on the earthly plane, was in AD 1332, when the Knights Templar were destroyed by the French King Philip the Fair, in league with Pope Clement V. The Templars' task was to establish a new Christian social order in Europe, and as its spiritual and moral authority grew, it threatened both the Vatican and the King. The hand of the Sun Demon in the destruction of the Templars was revealed when Philip ordered the Knights tortured, and they confessed to unspeakable blasphemies. These confessions actually described the temptations posed by the demonic servants of Sorath, which the Templars had, in their initiatory path, successfully resisted.

Steiner, who died in 1925 before Bolshevism had reached it most terrifying excesses, and before Nazism had come to power, laid the groundwork for others to discover the fulfillment of the occult law of recapitulation as it played out in the twentieth century: Sorath's attack on humanity at Gondhishapur rippled through time to land on the twentieth century shore in 1917 as the Bolshevik Revolution, while Philip the Fair's Sorath-inspired attack on the Templars was echoed again in 1933 when the Nazis seized power and began their twelve-year reign of terror.

As the twentieth century—history's bloodiest—drew to a close, many people the world over looked with delight or dread toward the year 2000. For the Sun Demon, the millennial year was incidental, for his number—1998, the third occurrence of Sorath's 666— preceded it, and would pre-empt any celebrations humanity might be planning.

The celebrants at the Champlain and Hudson-Fulton commemorations saw the twentieth century as a culmination of history, a glorious apotheosis of human invention, discovery, and achievement. Rudolf Steiner also saw a culmination in the twentieth century—a culmination of the adversarial powers' plan to take humanity off of its destined course toward reuniting with the Sun Spirit, come back to Earth in an etheric form for all humanity. The twentieth century would offer a trial for humanity that would quicken at century's end, with the third reappearance in the Christian era of the number 666—the number of the Beast of the Apocalypse. John's *Apocalypse* identifies three Beasts: a great red dragon in heaven with 7 heads, 10 horns, and 7 crowns; a Beast from the sea with 7 heads, 10 horns, and 10 crowns—like a leopard with bear's feet and a lion's mouth; and a Beast from the earth, with two-horns, looking like a lamb but speaking like a dragon. This last Beast is the one whose number is 666, who resembles the Christ, but is a deception—the Antichrist. Like the Apocalypticist John, Rudolf Steiner's teachings outlined a stark choice for human beings in the twentieth century—between the Lamb or the two-horned Beast. And as John had written, when the Antichrist appeared, it would be a threefold attack, with Sorath supporting and inspiring the evil workings of Lucifer and Ahriman.

In his 1909 lecturing activity, Steiner had often spoken of how, at the Transfiguration, Christ stood between the Old Testament figures of Elijah—embodying strength—and Moses, who embodied wisdom. Steiner's exegesis of the Bible always was mindful of a similar threefold arrangement in the New Testament; Christ's stance between the disciples Peter and John was an image of two different streams of Christianity—the exoteric church of Peter, which has tended to harden into static, imprisoning dogma; and the esoteric church of John—the mystical, revolutionary stream that had stayed mostly subterranean for nineteen centuries, but with the end of the Kali Yuga and Rudolf Steiner's appearance as a spiritual teacher, had come into the open. A final threefold pattern that Rudolf Steiner frequently spoke of was that of Christ and His two heavenly disciples—Michael, the Archangel of the Sun; and Gabriel, the Archangel of the Moon. In the seventh century, at the first occurrence of Sorath's number, Steiner indicated that the Moon religion of Islam, inspired by Gabriel, had played a crucial role in blocking much of the Sorath-inspired knowledge poised to flood Europe from the Academy of Gondishapur. In 1332, the Archangel Michael, who had aided the Knights Templar from the spiritual world, assured that the Templar stream of esoteric Christianity did not die out with the assassinations of the individual Knights.

The "threefoldness" of the earth and cosmos was a constant leitmotif in Steiner's work, and underlay also his understanding of a larger rhythm of time. Steiner always called the period of Christ's incarnation, the "Turning Point in Time." Christ's life stood then as a fulcrum between two other incarnations—of Lucifer and Ahriman. Lucifer, the adversarial spirit of expansion, had around 3000

BC taken on an actual incarnation in China, in an attempt to fore-stall humanity's full *incarnation* into the physical Earth, which was necessary for human freedom. Ahriman, the dark spirit of contraction, brought the opposite impulse to bear, and since the fifteenth century had attempted to derail humanity's destined path toward spiritual *excarnation*. While historical symmetry might suggest that Ahriman's physical incarnation would not be due until 3000 years *after* Christ, Steiner never failed to point out how Ahriman was a being whose activity was characterized by bringing certain impulses too soon, ahead of their time. This was clearly Ahriman's task in 666, with Sorath's help bringing advanced technology to the scholars at Gondhishapur. If Steiner's indication of an imminent incarnation of Ahriman in America was correct, it would mean that Ahriman arrived 1000 years "too early," but, given his nature, the year 1998 offered a perfect opportunity.

The twentieth century was a moment of opportunity for Sorath precisely *because* the very accomplishments championed by the tercentenary celebrations—modern technologies of electricity, lighting, wireless telegraphy, flight, steam power, and, standing behind all of these, the worldview of materialism—were the outward expressions of infernal powers. Sorath, Steiner taught, will not enter into a physical incarnation, but always remains as a sort of spiritual shadow. The signature of that shadow within human history has always been and will always be the activity of black magic. In his 1909 lectures on John's *Apocalypse*, Steiner repeatedly referred to previous periods of human history—from ancient Atlantis to the Persian, Egyptian, and Greco-Roman eras—when black magical activity caused catastrophe.

Like all "white" magicians, Rudolf Steiner knew intimately the reality of black magic, yet he almost never gave specifics about its nature. Just speaking of such matters ran the risk of stirring the demons into motion. For those best acquainted with Steiner's work, they knew black magic to be any efforts against the Divine plan for humanity and the Earth, which was for the Earth to "become a Sun." Through the conscious, self-directed spiritual evolution of human beings, the Earth too would be spiritualized, and in the future would reunite with the Sun. Possessing no creative power of its own, black magic could only exploit the Divine Will by inverting and demonizing it. The goal of Earth evolution, Rudolf Steiner always taught, was Love; humanity was to turn Earth into a planet of Love. Despite any momentary efflorescence of good will, peace, and human harmony displayed in the 1909 celebrations, America's Venus was in eclipse, and Mars was surely on the rise.

5

CLOTHED WITH THE SUN, THE MOON UNDER HER FEET

IN EARLY TWENTIETH CENTURY PARLANCE, at a time when Satan had lost all "beingness" in secular America, the phrase "black magic" was bandied about casually, indicative of how skeptical people were that magic—black or white—actually existed. If one looked up "magic" in the dictionary in 1909, one found that the emphasis was on pretense and illusion: "Any pretended or supposed supernatural art of putting into action the power of spirits" (*Standard Dictionary*); "Any supposed supernatural act, especially the pretended art of controlling the actions of spiritual beings." (*Century Dictionary*) With all magic now "pretended or supposed," America at the opening of the twentieth century was even losing the memory of its own rich history of magic. In 1907, when George Lyman Kittredge published his *Notes on Witchcraft,* the monograph took it for granted that there had been no actual magical activity at Salem in 1692. Kittredge had just become president of the American Folklore Society, and despite his extensive acquaintance with anecdotes of magic, he attributed them all to "fantasy" and "imagination."

In Hudson and Champlain's day, European and native alike saw each other as agents of the devil, if not demons themselves. Adrian van der Donck, interviewing a number of men and women who had witnessed Hudson's arrival, found that "they knew not what to make of [the Dutch], and could not comprehend whether they came down from Heaven, or whether they were Devils." Seeing the painted faces of the men on shore, Hudson and his shipmates wondered if "it were not the Devil himself." In the seventeenth century, Algonquians and Europeans also encountered devils in forms other than themselves. Van der Donck wrote that "they have a great dread of the Devil, who gives them wonderful trouble," but that they insisted that their devils would "have nothing to do with the Dutch." Describing Algonquin shamans, Champlain said that they "speak to the Devil face to face and he tells them what they must do, both in war and other affairs. . . . Moreover they believe all the dreams they dream are true; and indeed there are many of them who say that they have seen in dreams things which happen or will happen. But to speak the truth about them, these are visions of the Devil, who deceives and misleads them."

At the Tercentenary celebrations, what little knowledge there may once have been about the thought worlds of the native peoples had mostly vanished, replaced by elaborate displays of the material culture, as uncovered by archaeology. At the American Museum of Natural History, half of the Plains Indian Hall was taken over for an exhibition entitled "The Indians of Manhattan Island and Vicinity." There were stone implements, pottery, bone and antler tools, and trade items from a dozen sites on Staten Island, including a section reconstructing graves excavated at Tottenville. A couple of skeletons were displayed with arrow points that had been found puncturing the bones. Representing Manhattan Island, there were archaeological remains from Fort Washington, Cold Spring, Inwood Station, the Harlem Ship Canal, and the Academy Street Garden. Though most of the artifacts came from recent excavations in the northern, less populated part of Manhattan, some of the objects came from places now at the heart of the metropolis. Shell artifacts were displayed from a site at the junction of Bowery and Canal Streets; a grooved stone axe found at 77th and Avenue B; an arrowhead from 81st Street and Hudson River Drive.

The Museum published a 300-page monograph to accompany the exhibition, which included a report from ethnologist Frank Speck that gave a bit of life to the catalogue of mute stones and bones uncovered from the earth. Speck—who had just gotten his Ph.D. in anthropology under Franz Boas at Columbia—wrote up the ethnography of the Mohegan and Niantic Indians, persisting as a community right into the early twentieth century in nearby Connecticut. Speck was fascinated by (and believed in the efficacy of) witchcraft and magic, and Mrs. Fidelia Fielding, a Mohegan woman who had died the year before at the age of 80, had obliged him with many tales of the supernatural from her youth. Mrs. Fielding told Speck that a *moigu*—a witch—was anyone who was known to have communication with supernatural powers. Such persons were inclined to malicious actions believed to be accomplished with the help of the Devil, and so they were avoided. How their magical powers were acquired was not known to Mrs. Fielding, but she insisted that "a wizard is not long in being found out by his magic." That magic included instantly transporting themselves from place to place; achieving personal desires by special individual magic; concocting charms for casting spells over persons, animals, and things; and also affecting the cure of certain diseases. She told Speck that "the time of the witches or shamans is past," that, since the taking up of Christianity, the witches had gone off. The last one had been Israel Freeman, who magically deformed the faces of two wives of whom he had grown jealous. Freeman, who was always being snarled at by dogs, could instantly quiet them by pointing a handful of weeds in their direction.

This was magic of a quite minor sort, hardly the sort of black magic that Rudolf Steiner spoke of when he warned of the doings of Sorath. But America had seen episodes of horrific black magic in its own past. In 1909, Frank Speck's Columbia University colleague Manuel Gamio, another Boas student, began the first controlled excavations at Teotihuacan, the ancient ruins outside of Mexico City, where he would eventually uncover the sculptured heads of the rain god Tlaloc and the feathered serpent Quetzalcoatl—complete with obsidian eyes and enameled fangs. According to Steiner, there in the Valley of Mexico had once taken place the most grisly black magical practices:

> An Ahrimanic, caricatured counterpart appeared in the West . . . [who] was called by a name that sounded something like Taotl. Taotl was thus an Ahrimanic distortion of the "Great Spirit"—a mighty being and one who did not descend to physical incarnation. A great many men were initiated into the mysteries of Taotl but the initiation was of a completely Ahrimanic

character.... When a candidate had been initiated in the correct way, the teaching concerning the secrets of the cosmos was then imparted to him ... [but] the wisdom was imparted to no one who had not previously committed a murder in a particular manner.... The one to be murdered was laid out on a structure that was reached by one or two steps running along each side. This scaffold-like structure, a kind of catafalque, was rounded off above and when the victim was laid upon it, he was bent strongly back. This special way of being bound to the scaffold forced his stomach outward so that with one cut, which the initiate had been prepared to perform, it could be cut out.... When the stomach had been excised, it was offered to the god Taotl, again with special ceremonies.

The spiritual effect of these murders, according to Steiner, was that the sacrificial victim's soul was driven away from the Earth, into the realm of Lucifer—the Eighth Sphere. At the same time, the "initiate"—i.e., murderer—was bound to the victim, and could receive knowledge from the spiritual world.

These "revolting" Ahrimanic mystery practices were ultimately aimed at creating an entire culture oriented toward fleeing the Earth. To prevent this from happening, another set of mysteries, with its own initiation practices, was established to counteract the Taotl mysteries:

These were mysteries in which a being lived who did not come down to physical incarnation but also could be perceived by men gifted with a certain atavistic clairvoyance when they had been prepared. This being was Tezcatlipoca.... The teachings of Tezcatlipoca soon escaped from the mysteries and were spread abroad exoterically.... Another spirit was set up against [Tezcatlipoca] who, for the Western Hemisphere, had much in common with the spirit whom Goethe described as Mephistopheles. He was indeed his kin. This spirit was designated with a word that sounded like Quetzalcoatl.... Quetzalcoatl also never appeared directly incarnated.

As if this story were not incredible enough, Steiner went on to tell how these two supersensible beings then worked through two historical individuals: He spoke first of a man called "Vitzliputzli," who had been born of a virgin, in the year AD 1. Hinting that he had researched this thoroughly in the Akashic record, Steiner further stated that at the same time, another man was born, who had in previous incarnations been an initiate in the Taotl/Quetzalcoatl mysteries, and who was thus "one of the greatest black magicians, if not the greatest ever to tread the earth; he possessed the greatest secrets that are to be acquired on this path."

This black magician, at the age of 30, had acquired a power so tremendous that he would have been able to detour human evolution. To prevent this, Vitzliputzli, the son of the virgin, after battling for three years against the unnamed black magician:

> was able to have the great magician crucified, and not only through the crucifixion to annihilate his body but also to place his soul under a ban, by this means rendering its activities powerless as well as its knowledge. Thus the knowledge assimilated by the great magician of Taotl was killed. In this way Vitzliputzli was able to win again for earthly life all those souls who, as indicated, had already received the urge to follow Lucifer and leave the earth. Through the mighty victory he had gained over the powerful black magician, Vitzliputzli was able to imbue men again with the desire for earthly existence and successive incarnations.

This crucifixion by Vitzlipuzli of the black magician had thus occurred *in the year 33—the year of Christ's crucifixion at Golgotha.*

When Steiner told this remarkable story, archaeologists were still working out the chronological sequence of cultures in the Valley of Mexico. A great deal was of course known about the Mexica (the name the people called themselves; "Aztec" became widely used in the 19th century by English-speaking students of the region) people as a result of their conquest after 1519 by the Spanish, but the peoples who had preceded them were a complete enigma. Even the Mexica, when they arrived in 1325 at Lake Texcoco and began to build their capital city of Tenochtitlan, were dumbfounded by the ruins at Teotihuacan, which had been abandoned centuries before.

From the eyewitness accounts of the conquistadors, the world had long known of the Aztec empire's barbaric culture of death, of the "Flower Wars" waged against their neighbors in order to secure captives for sacrifice to the Sun God Huitzilopochtli (i.e., Steiner's "Vitzliputzli"). But the relationship of the Aztec, and the culture of heart sacrifice centered at their capital city of Tenochtitlan, to the ruins of Teotihuacan—the "City of the Gods"—just a couple of dozen miles away, was unknown. This was one of the principal questions that Manuel Gamio hoped to answer with his excavations. In the Hall of Mexico at the American Museum, there were many spectacular objects—most notably a full-scale plaster cast of the famous Aztec calendar stone, which had been discovered in 1790. But the new Hall was mute about the calendar of cultural development in the Valley of Mexico.

In *Aztec* myth, Huitzilopochtli was the god who instituted both the ritual of heart sacrifice and the imperial wars that they were designed to support. Quetzalcoatl was the god who spoke out *against* heart sacrifice and cannibalism. In Steiner's story, the gods Huitzilopochtli and the black magician inspired by Quetzalcoatl were actually physically incarnated human beings, *but their identities were reversed from the Aztec myth*. In addition, it was well known from the accounts of the conquistadors that the Aztec had practiced *heart sacrifice*, and yet Steiner kept referring to the excision of the *stomach*. One more seeming discrepancy is that crucifixion was not known (and still is not) to be a form of sacrifice or torture found in Mesoamerica at this time. Steiner was not particularly well read in the history of Mesoamerica; his countryman Eduard Seler, who had never set foot in Mexico, was perhaps the leading authority on Mesoamerican myth, and Steiner had read some of Seler's work, but this narrative that he divulged was clearly read from the Akashic record, not from between the lines of contemporary scholarship. A few details of Steiner's story do fit what was known from Aztec myth: the principal gods named by Steiner— Huitzilopochtli, Quetzalcoatl, Tezcatlipoca—are those of the Aztec and pre-Aztec cultures of the region; Huitzilopochtli was born of a virgin, the goddess Coatlicue, who, in the myth, had conceived after being touched on the shoulder by a ball of feathers.

Steiner made a very brief remark that linked the ancient culture of Teotihuacan with the more recent Tenochtitlan of the Aztec, when he said that the black magical mysteries of the first century AD were:

> subsequently revived, however, and history tells of the fate suffered by numerous Europeans who went to America after the discovery of that continent. Many Europeans met their death at the hands of Mexican priest-initiates who bound them to scaffold-like structures and cut out their stomachs with expert skill. This is a matter of historical knowledge, and it was an aftermath of what I have been describing to you.

In saying "aftermath," Steiner seemed to be suggesting that the black magical activities of the Aztec at the time of the Spanish arrival in Tenochtitlan (1519) were a true continuation of the earlier culture of black magic. Steiner saw a much deeper ancestry to both these episodes of black magic in America though, saying that they were "revivals" of the black magical practices that had developed in ancient Atlantean times and had ultimately brought that period of human history to an end.

The overall arc of the lecture series had been characteristically wide-ranging: beginning with a discussion of the spiritual effects of Greek and Roman civilization, Steiner had continued with a lecture on the Lucifer-inspired teacher/counselor of Genghis Khan, saying that the discovery in the fifteenth century of North America—a continent strong in Ahrimanic forces—was a necessary counterbalance to Asia's Luciferic tendency to draw human beings away from the Earth; then came an indictment of Spiritualism's claim that the experiences they described were received from spirits of the dead; a description of Goethe's *Fairy Tale of the Green Snake and the Beautiful Lily* as an expression of the *true* path of humanity in the current era; and finally, a lecture on how Henry VIII's divorce battle with Rome had led to the founding of the Anglican Church. When Rudolf Steiner gave the third lecture, "The After Effects of the Atlantean Mysteries in America and Asia," his audience was so confused that he had to repeat its principle points a few days later.

The day after this repetition, Steiner gave a lecture entitled "The

CLOTHED WITH THE SUN, THE MOON UNDER HER FEET   99

Cosmic Knowledge of the Knights Templar," in which he characterized the Templar initiation practices and their resulting wisdom as
Luciferic, and said that their adversary Philip the Fair's attack upon
them had been inspired by Ahriman. In fact, Philip's burning desire
for the Templars' gold, and his brutal interrogations of the Templars
was itself a form of Ahrimanic initiation that had given the French
king the same order of knowledge as that engendered by the Mexican initiates in their practices of torture. Given Steiner's statements
about the dark practices that had brought on the Atlantean catastrophe, torture was clearly the perennial black heart of Ahrimanic/
Sorathean magic. In this same lecture, Steiner drew a picture on the
blackboard of the Earth, with lines representing the convergence of
magnetic currents in North America. In the southern hemisphere,
Steiner made an S-shaped magnetic line, saying that this was the
region of Lemuria, and that although people failed to notice it any
longer, magnetism was like a force "vivifying the earth." He then
quoted from "Ahasver," an 1838 poem by Julius Mosen:

> In line direct and straight from Southern Pole
> Takes the Magnetic Line its chosen course,
> When suddenly it twines in serpent-curve
>
> There before India and its neighbor isles
> Before the dungeon where in deepest woe
> Sits the Eternal Mother ever bound.
>
> In circle form the Line drew back its length,
> And twining swift and secret on itself
> With a single plunge in swirling vortex fell.
>
> There the Great Spirit in a first embrace
> Held the poor spouse, and from their ardent fire
> Sprang the Earth-demons instantly to life.
>
> When thus the first creation came to naught,
> The Great, the Nameless Spirit in his wrath
> Stamped down the bridal couch beneath the sea.

Steiner never again spoke of the first century magical battle in
Mexico, and, especially within the context of these elliptical lectures

with their far-flung themes and topics, it is difficult to fathom the reason for his having done so at that particular moment in 1916. As surely as that June 29, 1908 lecture on Sorath or the January 1, 1909 lecture on Mephistopheles and earthquakes, though, Steiner's revelation of the magical battle in ancient Mexico was made for a particular purpose. Taken alone, the implications of his brief narrative of the AD 33 crucifixion of the black magician were revolutionary: the synchronicity of the magical battle in Mexico with the events in Palestine drew the Western Hemisphere and its people into the Christian myth as critical historical actors, not centuries *after* the Mystery of Golgotha, but at the very same moment. Embedded as this story was within an epic historical sweep from Atlantis and Lemuria, through classical Greece and Rome, to Genghis Khan's thirteenth century conquest of Asia, the fourteenth century crushing of the Knights Templar, and fifteenth century discovery of America, the story also called out to be heard as *present* reality as much as past event.

One constant of Steiner's teaching was that the human consciousness was the true plane upon which history unfolded, and that *all* outer deeds and events were the "footprints" of consciousness—and thus spiritual—evolution. Simultaneously aided and hindered by the supersensible beings Lucifer and Ahriman, humanity had muddled through the middle of eternity to land in the twentieth century with the potential for vast new understandings. Yet, as was clear from this lecture series and many others given by Rudolf Steiner, humanity had repeatedly succumbed to the temptation toward black magic. In the fog-shrouded mists of ancient Atlantis, the Persian desert in AD 666, and the fields of southern France in 1332, the Beast had surfaced from the depths, finding human beings who were happy to unite themselves with him. By telling this story of Huitzilopochtli's battle at the Turning Point in Time with Quetzalcoatl, the "Feathered Serpent," Steiner consciously positioned America as a collaborator in the history of black magic, and for those who had ears to hear, that history was not over yet.

Burlington

At the top of the long hill leading up from Burlington's waterfront was the Queen City's version of the American Museum of Natural History. On any day of the Tercentenary week one could stop by Torrey Hall at the University of Vermont to view the University Museum. If the doors were locked and the janitor couldn't be found, one walked over to the Billings Library and asked the librarian for a key. Founded in 1825 by George Wyllys Benedict, Professor of Mathematics and Natural Philosophy, the museum had as its main objective the collection of the standard furred, feathered, and finned natural history fare, but it soon came to serve as a repository of anything considered remotely exotic. Thanks to the acquisitiveness of UVM alumni and peripatetic Burlingtonians, the little museum received lava from Mount Vesuvius, plaster casts of Greek and Roman coins, a Greek dress brought back by Captain J. P. Miller of Montpelier who had just returned from his exploits in the Greek War for Independence, even local curiosities like the piece of fossil wood which Alvah Foote discovered while digging a well not half a mile from the campus. Bits and pieces of aboriginal North American culture flowed steadily into the collection: a Sioux dog-harness, Inuit artifacts from the coast of Labrador, the "complete dress of an Indian chief" collected by Major Ethan Allen Hitchcock, and arrowheads picked up by local farmers every spring.

The trickle of prehistoric artifacts from the surrounding area grew after 1870, when Professor George Henry Perkins arrived at UVM. The Yale Ph.D. had plenty of opportunity for contact with Vermont's small army of amateur natural historians, first as promoter with the State Agricultural College at UVM, then as State Entomologist (1880–1895) and State Geologist (1898–1933). In between recruiting farmers' sons for the agriculture course, lecturing to Grange clubs on successful manuring or the dangers of apple borers, or inquiring after promising fossil localities, Perkins would often find himself invited to view a farmer's personal museum. In boxes or spread out on tables all over the state were collections of archaeological material—stone spear points, atlatl weights, axes, knives and hammers, shards of pottery. Judge A. B. Halbert, whose

farm was on Abbey Brook in Essex, plowed up hundreds of arrowheads and collected others on travels that took him to Wisconsin,
California, and north to the Saint Lawrence. When he died in 1874,
his widow gave his collection of over 1000 specimens to the
museum. In 1878, John Norton Pomeroy, whose property ran down
from North Prospect Street onto the eastern edge of the Intervale,
the broad floodplain flanking the Winooski River, gave the museum
an earthenware jar dug up from a cave in Bolton. Throughout the
late nineteenth century, Dr. David Sherwood Kellogg, a UVM alum-
nus living across the lake in Plattsburgh, first donated (and later
sold) duplicates from his collections to the museum. Miss Anne E.
Porter sent artifacts she picked out of the sand as she went for walks
on the dunes at Colchester Point. Elihu Taft brought armloads of
stone implements from his local collecting, and along with his son
and daughter, sent back pottery from Zuni pueblo, tule mats from
the Salish of Puget Sound, and even Eskimo material.

At the center of this frenzied acquisitiveness was George Henry
Perkins, and at the center of his enormous appetite for the natural
world was an abiding interest in Vermont's Indians. Perkins pot-
hunted sites around Swanton with Lester Truax in the 1880s, appar-
ently never communicating with any of the region's living Abenaki.
He acknowledged their presence, but refused them their indige-
nousness, referring to the Swanton (Mississquoi) Abenaki as "survi-
vors of the St. Francis tribe." There is a photo of Perkins and Truax
in camp together in Swanton, proudly displaying fish they have
caught, with their tent in the background, looking for all the world
like a couple of Indians. Any good Swanton citizen who stumbled
on them might have taken them for such.

The second edition (1913) of the Champlain Tercentenary's *Final
Report* concluded with George Perkins's "Notes on the Archaeology
of the Champlain Valley." In his attempt to understand the native
people in the region in 1609, at the time of European contact, Perkins –like his counterparts at the American Museum of Natural
History—moved back and forth between what he knew about
recent, even living, Indian peoples, and what the objects dug from
the earth said about their ancestors. One site in particular fascinated Perkins—an ancient burial ground in Swanton, where in 1860

Deacon Elliott Frink opened a number of graves below a stand of white pines on his land. Deacon Frink and another Swanton man eventually opened some 25 graves in the sand, and gathered up what bones remained along with a wealth of grave goods. Most of their collection wound up in the State Museum in Montpelier, where Perkins examined it. What struck him was how different the artifacts were from those with which he was familiar from the region. That they had been fashioned by some other people was shown, Perkins argued, "by the character of the articles found, as they differ in many respects from those taken from the graves of the St. Francis tribe, being of finer material for the most part, of different shape, more elaborately wrought and altogether giving evidence of a higher degree of culture than that to which the Iroquois or Algonquins attained." There were copper bars, shell beads, and a series of objects that were a complete mystery. One was a gnarled and knobby knot of pine root that looked like a carving. In one grave was found a beautiful water-worn cobble of white quartz, one side of which had been covered in red ochre. A few pieces of fossil-bearing rock were also found in the graves. Hollow, cylindrical stone shafts, called "blocked-end tubes" by Perkins, were thought perhaps to be pipes, but there was no evidence of burning inside them. One of these tubes bore a carving of a Thunderbird that he interpreted as a crude representation of a "fish hawk," or osprey. The tube was actually a shaman's curing device, used for sucking out the pollutants that caused sickness. The Thunderbird—which shared certain mythological characteristics with Quetzalcoatl—inscription was an aid to the tool's efficacy.

There were also on the tube a series of markings that another examiner had declared to be akin to the magical marks of the Eleusinian mystery rites, and evidence that the maker must have been an ancient Hebrew. Perkins dismissed such speculation, believing instead that the makers had been "some branch of the mound-building race [who] wandered eastward." Perkins reasoned that since they had built no mounds, there had been only a few of them, who had stayed in the region very briefly. While the copper, the white beads, and the Thunderbird never moved Perkins to imagine the mythical world of the people who made them, he was titillated by the possibility that "the primeval forests of Vermont witnessed those awful rites of the mound-builders, those human sacrifices to the sun god."

In Perkins day, there was much speculation that the Mound-builders were the northern representatives of the imperial, sacrificial cultures of Mesoamerica. Perkins had never been to the Valley of Mexico, but he had seen the "Aztec Village" on the Midway at the World's Columbian Exposition in Chicago in 1893. The recreated village (which was actually based on a Mayan village in the Yucatan, suggesting how murky popular notions of Mesoamerica were at the turn of the century) was enormously popular, nearly as popular as the attraction next door—the "Electric Scenic Theater," which used lighting effects to take the visitor through an imaginary day in the Swiss Alps. The mock ruins, painted frescoes, and plaster reproductions of statues and artifacts in the Aztec Village were also meant to transport the visitor out of time and space, to some unspecified moment before Cortes arrived in 1519. Though there were no artifacts for sale at the Aztec Village, Perkins was able to buy objects for his museum at the anthropological exhibits. From some Kwakiutl men and women—organized by Franz Boas for the exhibit, they shared the building with Apaches, Navajo, four Penobscot families in birch bark wigwams, Iroquois in a longhouse, and Arawaks in thatched huts—Perkins bought a wooden mask and a copper bracelet for $2.50 each; a bird whistle for $1.50; and a throwing stick and a model canoe for 75¢ apiece.

While most visitors to the University Museum viewed these objects without any form of narrative context, students in Perkins' anthropology course had an opportunity to hear how the skulls, spears, and other exotica might be fit into a larger scheme. A central feature of the course was Perkins' use of archaeological and ethnological material from the museum to illustrate the peoples and themes he discussed. As Perkins understood it, anthropology was above all a study of origins; "There is no such thing as chance. There is a cause, a 'why' for all we do." In his first lecture, he gave as an example the simple gesture of a man taking off his hat to a woman, whose origin he said was that of the knight removing his helmet to signify that he came in peace. He then sketched contemporary theories about the origins of modern civilization, that man was originally "a very low savage" and either "retrograded" or "advanced" toward a state of modern civilization.

In order to show this progress and growth, Perkins, by way of the museum collection, developed a baseline measure of savagery to contrast with the Aryan Peoples, who were "a great nation, [and] rule the world." Savagery was first and foremost characterized by brutality, and Perkins could demonstrate this handily by the many weapons in the museum. In Perkins' lectures, Africa, the cradle of humanity, was also the cradle of inhumanity. He began with the Africans of the Great Desert, who were "dark-skinned, [had] motley hair, thick lips, and long arms." Governed by a despotic chief, these savages were characterized by "brutality, [and] indolence every-where." Their "mental capacity [was] low." Nearer the equator were the "dwarf tribes, pygmies, who were better looking than others," but were "great fighters ... [and] cruel." Further south were the Bushmen, who were "lean and ill-favored, hairy, rudimentary," and couldn't "talk right." Hottentots were "superior," because they dwelled in permanent houses and were "jolly, good-natured." The tribes of the Nile valley—the Baris, Nuer, and Dinka—were "cheery, fond of display, and cruel to each other." The most popular African show-and-tell was Perkins' lecture on the Zulu. He brought along a variety of spears, clubs, and cowhide shields that had been given to the museum by Reverend Lewis Grout of Brattleboro, who had spent fifteen years as a missionary at Umsunduzi in the southern Africa nation of Natal. Grout had gone there with his new wife in 1846 to convert the heathen savages and bring light to the "Dark Continent."

Not just Africa, but the whole world was filled with savages. Tibetans, who were amply illustrated by Henry LeGrand Cannon's collection in the museum, were "rude, uncouth." The Manchu "lead a semibarbarous and romantic life." The Tungus of Siberia were "still ruder and wilder people." Perkins found fierceness and rude-ness among Tartans, Finns, Lapps, Estonians, Eskimo, Japanese, and Koreans. But it was the last stop on the worldwide tour that took the students the deepest into the heart of darkness. Amongst the "Insular and Littoral Peoples" were found the Papuans, who were large, skillful at making canoes and *tapu* cloth, and whose elaborately carved war clubs Perkins brought to class. He also brought examples of their poisoned arrows, which the fierce Papuan warriors threw into "putrid human flesh."

The principal text for Perkins' course in anthropology was Edward Burnett Tylor's two-volume *Primitive Culture* (1871), and while the entire second volume elaborates Tylor's understanding of magical thinking, and Tylor had a particular interest in the anthropology of sacrifice (in associating Christianity's sacrificial conception of Jesus' death with the barbarism of primitive cultures' sacrificial rites, Tylor hoped to de-legitimize Christianity) he says little there about either the Aztec or prior sacrificial systems. And he is completely shy about relating Aztec myth and their elaborate practice of heart sacrifice. He says about Huitzilopochtli that it would be presumptuous "to attempt a general solution of this inextricable compound parthenogenetic deity." For his understandings of Quetzalcoatl and Tezcatlipoca, Tylor relied on the Franciscan friar Bernardino de Sahagun, who arrived in Mexico in 1529, and who through his missionary work with the Aztec over the next half-century, became the premier European student of the Mexican mind.

By the late nineteenth century, there had been published two English translations of Sahagun's *General History of the Things of New Spain*; a more helpful source is the Dominican friar Diego Duran's *History of the Indies of New Spain*. Growing up in Mexico City just a generation after the Conquest, Duran had heard grisly tales of the old Mexican mystery rites; in his *History* he describes a ceremony on a feast day of Huitzilopochtli:

> Smeared with black, the six sacrificers appeared. . . . Seeing them come out . . . filled all the people with dread and terrible fear! The high priest carried in one hand a large stone knife, sharp and wide. Another carried a wooden yoke carved in the form of a snake. They humbled themselves before the idol and then stood in order next to a pointed stone, which stood in front of the door of the idol's chamber. The stone was so high that it reached one's waist. And it was so sharp that when the

sacrificial victim had been stretched across it on his back he was bent in such a way that if the knife was dropped upon his chest it split open with the ease of a pomegranate.

Duran continues his narrative:

All the prisoners of war who were to be sacrificed upon this feast were then brought forth. . . . Surrounded by guards . . . the victims were forced to ascend to the long platform . . . all of them totally nude. . . . [The priests] seized the victims one by one, one by one foot, another by the other, one priest by one hand, and another by the other hand. The victim was thrown on his back, upon the pointed stone, where the wretch was grabbed by the fifth priest, who placed the yoke upon his throat. The high priest then opened the chest and with amazing swiftness tore out the heart, ripping it out with his own hands. Thus steaming, the heart was lifted toward the sun, and the fumes were offered up to the sun. The priest then turned toward the idol and cast the heart in its face. After the heart had been extracted, the body was allowed to roll down the steps of the pyramid. . . . After they had been slain and cast down, their owners—those who had captured them—retrieved the bodies. They were carried away, distributed, and eaten, in order to celebrate. . . .

When Perkins visited the Aztec Village on the Midway at the Chicago World's Fair, most of the spectators came because they knew the reputation of the Aztec as barbaric torturers, but few if any had ever read the eyewitness accounts of Aztec sacrifice. Duran concluded his description:

The sacrifice ended when all the victims had been slain. Their blood was sprinkled generously upon . . . the pieces of dough which represented the flesh and the bones of the god. All were now consecrated with human blood. . . . Then this and the parts which represented its bones and flesh were broken up into small fragments. Beginning with the elders, everyone received communion with this *tzoalli* [dough]—old and young, men and women, old men and children. All received it with such reverence, awe, and joy that truly it was a thing of wonder! The people claimed that they had eaten the flesh and the bones of the gods, though they were unworthy. . . .

Duran stated that when the Spaniards severely criticized the sacrificial rite, the Aztecs made "indifferent or sarcastic remarks". They insisted that the sacrifice of human beings was "the honored oblation of great lords and noblemen. They remember these things and tell of them as if they had been great deeds."

Elsewhere in Duran's chronicle one can find the key to the puzzle of the reversed identities of Quetzalcoatl and Huitzilopochtli. Duran, drawing from both oral accounts and Aztec manuscripts, tells of how, in 1428, a century after they first arrived at Lake Texcoco, the Aztecs, led by Izcoatl, defeated the Tepanecs, who had long dominated them. That same year, Izcoatl—at the insistence of his adviser/priest Tlacaellel—burned all the earlier codices, religious and historical documents. Tlacaellel then rewrote history to exalt the origins of the Aztecs and to establish a kind of divine imperial lineage through the Toltecs, who had also practiced human sacrifice. He reshaped the myth of Huitzilopochtli's virgin birth from Coatlicue, emphasizing the slaying of his 400 brothers and his sister Coyolxauhqui—the myth that became the foundation for the Aztec system of heart sacrifice and ritual dismemberment.

The present world of "the Fifth Sun" had begun, Tlacaellel argued, with the sacrifice of the gods at Teotihuacán; just as the gods had sacrificed themselves so the Sun would give man his life, so should man sacrifice himself so that the Sun could live. Only this could postpone the final cataclysm, and so Tlacaellel instituted the "Flower Wars"; Duran relates a dialogue between Tlacaellel and Moctezuma I, where Tlacaellel outlines the need to gain captives for sacrifice: "Our god will feed himself with them as though he were eating warm tortillas, soft and tasty, straight out of the oven. . . . And this war should be of such a nature that we do not endeavor to destroy the others totally. War must always continue, so that each time and whenever we wish and our god wishes to eat and feast, we may go there as one who goes to the market to buy something to eat . . . organized to obtain victims to offer our god Huitzilo-pochtli."

The name of Huitzilopochtli—the great initiate who in AD 33

defeated the black magical practices of the Quetzalcoatl initiates—
was after 1428 given to the God of War, and the system of heart sacrifice which Tlacaellel instituted was dedicated to this "Huitzilopochtli." Quetzalcoatl—the supersensible demonic entity whom
Steiner never identified exactly—was similarly inverted, recreated as
the benign culture hero, even to the point where the new myths
claimed that Quetzalcoatl had attempted to *end* the demonic practice of heart sacrifice.

The being called "Quetzalcoatl" by both the ancient Toltec and
the modern Mexica was and is identical with the being known in
Abrahamic traditions (Christianity, Judaism, and Islam) as Lucifer.
Even with all of the twisting that was done by Tlacaellel and the
Huitzilopochtli cult, the fundamental iconography of Quetzalcoatl
shows that he was perceived as a *serpent*, just as he was clairvoyantly
perceived in the ancient Abrahamic traditions. East and West, past
and present, the gods go by many names, but we can best know
their identity by the attributes that men give them. As the Dragon,
Lucifer had brought knowledge to human beings of Asia. He was
known there as *Tao*; in ancient Mexico, at the time of the Toltecs, he
was *Taotl*. And after 1428, for the Mexica, he was the "Plumed Serpent" Quetzalcoatl.

In the volcanic Valley of Mexico, the infernal powers bubbled up
like magma to institute a culture based on a counter-image of
Christ. This indeed is the hallmark of black magic, that always and
everywhere it appears it is only merely the *ape of God*, since it pos-
sesses no truly creative powers of its own. This aping—the menda-
cious inversion of the Good, the True, and the Beautiful—is written
all over the deeds of the Mexica empire. Tlacaellel stole and twisted
the story of Huitzilopochtli's virgin birth; stole and twisted the
story of Huitzilopochtli's vanquishing of the 400 Stars; stole Tezcatlipoca's preaching of a culture of love, and assigned it to the
adversary, Quetzalcoatl. Incredibly, outrageously, Tlacaellel completely reversed the qualities and deeds of the two gods and their
earthly representatives—Quetzalcoatl and the powerful black magician; Tezcatlipoca and Huitzilopochtli. Here is the signature of
Ahriman—the Lie. This lie substituted Ahriman—the post-Tlacllael
"Huitzilopochtli"—in place of Christ.

Rudolf Steiner had always called the modern era—the fifth 2160-year period after the end of Atlantis—the "Age of the Consciousness Soul," and he dated its beginning to the year 1414. Coming as it did but a scant 14 years later, the 1428 victory and subsequent reversal of the identities and qualities of the gods seemed one more attack on humanity at a critical turning point in history. That Izcoatl and Tlacaellel could so quickly and successfully turn black into white and white into black by inverting the identities of Huitzilopochtli and Quetzalcoatl seems wholly unbelievable . . . until one considers history. It took only a few centuries for Roman state power to co-opt Christ's teachings. Hitler led a modern Christian nation into a cult of death and terror in just a little over a decade. In fact, a close study of human history reveals how consistently evil masquerades as good, and how easily humanity joins the masquerade. And always, it begins with a myth—a *false* myth.

Rudolf Steiner hoped to counter that tendency, to offer a renewed understanding of ancient truths that were becoming ever harder for modern people to accept. He was in essence attempting to give humanity back its original, *true* myths. In those lectures in Cassel in 1909, Steiner had gone back to basics, working systematically through the very foundations of the Christian myth, to show how the Mystery of Golgotha sets in motion a mighty metamorphosis of the Earth. Two days after July 4th, 1909, he told his audience that "to produce the next phase of earth evolution. . . . Earth had to have a seed that could survive the death forces and overcome them":

> Since the event of Golgotha, a momentous process has been taking place in the universe. At the moment when the Cross was raised on Golgotha and the blood ran from the wounds of Christ Jesus, a new cosmic centre was created. We were there as human beings, whether in a physical body or out of it, between birth and death. Thus do new worlds arise. But one thing we must understand, that while we behold the dying Christ, we stand in the presence of the birth of a new Sun.

Christ united Himself with death which has become, on earth, the characteristic expression of the Father-Spirit. Christ goes to the Father and unites Himself with the expression of the Father—with death; thereby the image of death (as it has become) is shown in its falseness; for death now becomes the seed of a new Sun in the universe.

The seed needed to be planted *into* the Earth; Christ did this in descending into the underworld. At the time of His first coming, this was the period between the Crucifixion on Good Friday and the Resurrection on Easter Sunday—a period about which very little is said in the Gospels. At the time of the second coming, these momentous events were repeated in a new form—which Rudolf Steiner did not live to witness on the physical plane.

Steiner died in 1925, before the advent of the Etheric Christ, but the 12-year rhythm of Christ's descent to the Earth that had begun on the day of Steiner's birth—February 25, 1861—culminated on Ascension Day in 1932—April 25—after which Christ dwelled within the realm of humanity. Rather than experiencing the returned Christ in 1933, as Steiner had foreseen, the 12-year period that followed saw the reign of terror of Adolf Hitler. Myth is *always enacted on the plane of history,* and so it was that Christ—and humanity—suffered in the twentieth century a period comparable to the Passion of Good Friday in AD 33. World War II was a kind of second Crucifixion.

At the Mystery of Golgotha, Christ's descent into the underworld began as the constellation Virgo was rising—a sign that He was returning to the Mother. So it was at the time of the second coming that Christ's descent to the Mother began on Easter Night, March 31/April 1, 1945. While the stages of Christ's descent through the heavenly hierarchies was marked by the Jupiter rhythm connected to the planet's ingress into sidereal Leo, the stages of the descent into Hell are related to Jupiter's heliocentric ingress into sidereal Virgo, beginning on that Easter night in 1945. And just as the earthquake at the foot of the cross was the outer sign of Christ's descent into Hell at the Mystery of Golgotha, so the opening of the Earth's interior took place at the twentieth century second coming. On July 16, 1945, at the Trinity site in New Mexico, the first atomic bomb was exploded. Instead of turning the Earth into a spiritual Sun, as Christ's deed at Golgotha initiated, humanity took hold of the sub-earthly forces of Nature and produced an Ahrimanic caricature.

At 5:30 AM local time on July 16, atop a 60-foot-tall tower, "the gadget" (scientists' nickname for the bomb) exploded, leaving a crater of radioactive glass ten feet deep and 1100 feet wide. The surrounding mountains were illuminated "brighter than daytime" for one to two seconds. The shock wave from the explosion was felt over 100 miles away, as the mushroom cloud grew to reach over seven miles into the sky. Watching from ten miles southwest of the tower, J. Robert Oppenheimer recalled a line from Hindu scripture: "I am become Death, the destroyer of worlds."

Oppenheimer, who loved the poetry of John Donne, had chosen the name for the test site as he mused upon two of Donne's poems. Just before he died, Donne had written a "Hymn to God My God, in My Sicknesses," which contained the lines: "As West and East / In all flatt Maps—and I am one—are on, / So death doth touch the Resurrection." In the 14th of his Holy Sonnets, Donne had written: "Batter my heart, three person'd God," and this gave Oppenheimer the image of the Trinity.

Just southwest of the Trinity site, lies the Carrizozo Malpais, a 170 square mile lava field that is reached by the *Jornada del Muerto* ("Journey of the Dead Man"), the brutal and deadly 100-mile desert path once traveled by the Spanish conquistadores, and that later became the route across the boundary between New Spain and New Mexico. In a continuing, inexorable, but twisted enactment of myth on the plane of history, the Trinity site echoed not only the Mystery of Golgotha, but its mysterious counterpart that had played out in AD 33 in the Valley of Mexico. Rudolf Steiner had said that the Ahrimanized altars of the Taotl mysteries were a preparation for a future breach into the lower trinity—the three levels of threefold sub-earthly forces. Having opened the gates of Hell with their "gadget," Oppenheimer and his colleagues fulfilled the dark deeds begun by the black magicians of Quetzalcoatl. It was as if the blood shed by the centuries of black magical practices in the Valley of Mexico had seeped through the fissures in the volcanic soil, carrying its dark and destructive power, only to reemerge in the twentieth century at the lava fields a few hundred miles to the north, scientifically calculated, bureaucratically tamed, but black magic all the same.

BURLINGTON, 1909

In 1909, there was no one in Burlington better acquainted with the Valley of Mexico than Cyrus Guernsey Pringle, who in 1902 had moved from his East Charlotte farm to his home on the third floor of the Williams Science Hall on the University of Vermont campus. Called the "Prince of Plant Collectors" by Harvard botanist Asa Gray, Pringle had been spending a significant part of every year in Mexico since his first trip there in 1885, sent by Gray to collect plants in the state of Chihuahua. In subsequent years, collecting in 23 of Mexico's 32 states, Pringle and his assistant—he typically brought one of his young farmhands to help him collect—almost always spent some time botanizing around Mexico City.

Though a great modern city had grown up since the fall of Tenochtitlan, Pringle could still find within the confines of the Federal District native plants that would have been well known to the Aztec. In 1896, during an afternoon conducted around Lake Xochimilcho's canals and lagoons by a hired boatman, Pringle had discovered a new species of water lily that the Smithsonian Institution's Joseph Nelson Rose had named after him. It was one of dozens of Mexican plants bearing the specific epithet *pringlei*; in his 26 years of collecting in Mexico, Pringle discovered more new species than any collector in the history of botany. His journeys to Mexico could be said to have made the nation's flora known to the rest of the world.

Bearing a pass secured by Asa Gray from the Mexican Central Railroad owners in Boston, Pringle stepped on and off the trains whenever he caught promising glimpses of vegetation. Pringle always stayed in the Buena Vista quarter of the city, the modern, rapidly growing western end, with its open squares, and broad boulevards flanked by monuments and statues. It was but a mile walk to the Zocalo—situated atop Tenochtitlan's main sacrificial temple, the Templo Mayor dedicated to Huitzilopochtli—where Pringle could take the steam cars off in any direction. In Mexico City itself, Pringle's favorite collecting location was Chapultepec, where the first Aztec ruler Montezuma I, upon the counsel of Tlacaellel, had ordered his likeness inscribed into the volcanic rock.

1909 was an excellent year for Pringle, for it had begun with a reunion with his daughter, after having been separated for 37 years. In 1872, Pringle's wife—an itinerant Quaker evangelist who disapproved of her husband's deepening commitment to botanical collecting—had left him, taking their daughter. After years of trying to locate her, he had finally succeeded. In January 1909 he took the train south to Islip, Long Island and spent a week with his daughter and her family. He went for long walks with his grandson Clifford, and hunted for Virginia pine in the pitch pine woods.

Though he had been in Mexico for part of the winter, by mid-March he was back in Vermont, and spring found him collecting ladies slippers in Shelburne, shadbush in Burlington, violets in Colchester. On July 4, opening day of the Tercentenary, the 71-year-old Pringle was scampering along the cliffs at Hazen's Notch hunting for green alder, shrubby cinquefoil, and other rarities. In September he went back to Mexico for his last trip, and on September 26, the second day of the Hudson-Fulton celebration, he arrived in Mexico City. The very next day he headed out to one of his favorite places—the Cerro de Guadalupe—to collect wild potatoes on the upper slopes. To reach his destination, he had to first pass through the maze of churches, chapels, and cathedrals that ringed the bottom of the hill. He had on a previous visit been in to the main basilica, and seen there—though it was difficult, given that it was behind glass and at quite a distance from the altar rail—mounted in a gold frame Juan Diego's famous shawl, whose coarse cactus cloth, although over 350 years old, bore the vivid image of the Virgin.

Pringle was used to seeing the image of Nuestra Senora de Guadalupe everywhere he went in Mexico. She greeted him at every hotel reception desk when he checked in; she graced the doorways of the greatest mansions and the humblest hovels; on the trains, Mexican peasants and businessmen carried her image. There was not a soul in Mexico who did not know the story by heart. On December 9, 1531, the feast day of the Immaculate Conception of Mary, an Aztec widower named Cuauhtlatoatzin—called "Juan Diego" by the Franciscans who baptized him—was walking to church when he heard from the top of Tepeyac Hill an extraordinary chorus of songbirds, and someone calling his name in Nahuatl. Running up the hill, he saw coming out of the mists a beautiful woman, dressed like an Aztec princess. Calling him *Xocoyte*—"little son"—she asked him in his native language where he was going, and he answered by saying that he was on the way to celebrate the Virgin's feast day. The woman asked Juan Diego to tell the Bishop of Mexico, Juan de Zumarraga, that she wanted a *teocalli*—a sacred little house, to be built on the spot where she stood.

Juan Diego went to the bishop as instructed, but the Bishop, doubtful of the man's story, said that he needed some sign. Juan Diego returned to Tepeyac Hill and explained to the woman that the bishop did not believe him. After insisting he was not worthy and begging her to use another messenger, she instructed him to return to the Bishop, but still the skeptical Bishop demanded a sign. After she had promised one, he returned home to his uncle's house, and discovered him seriously ill. The next morning, concerned about his uncle's condition, he tried to skirt around Tepeyac hill, but again the woman stopped him, assuring him his uncle would not die. The woman, who referred to herself as *Coatlaxopeuh* (pronounced "Kwatlashupeh" the Nahuatl word means "She who crushes the serpent") asked Juan to climb the hill and gather flowers. Though it was December, when nothing would normally be in bloom, he found that the barren summit had been transformed into a garden, with roses from the region of Castile in Spain, the former home of Bishop Zumárraga. Coatlaxopeuh placed the roses carefully inside the folded tilma (cactus-fiber cloak) that Juan Diego wore and told him not to open it before anyone but the bishop. When Juan Diego unfolded his cloak before the Bishop, the roses cascaded out, revealing impressed upon the cloth an image of Coatlaxopeuh. The Bishop dropped to his knees before the image of the Virgin Mary.

Hearing "Coatlaxopeuh" as "Guadalupe," the Bishop recognized the image as *Nuestra Senora de Guadalupe,* a famous representation of the Virgin from his native region of Castile. The stars on her cloak, her dark face (the Guadalupe sculpture was one of Spain's Black Madonnas), the angel at her feet, her hands folded in prayer—all these features made the apparition meaningful to the Spanish. But when the story came back to Europe, *all* Europeans could recognize the symbolic language in the image. Her attire and hair-style was familiarly that of a woman from the Holy Land. The nimbus around Her and crescent moon below was a reminder of *Revelations* 12:1: "the Woman clothed with the Sun, the Moon under her feet." The red, white, and blue feathers on the wings of the supporting angel symbolized loyalty, faith, and fidelity; his position beneath Guadalupe indicates that She is his Queen. Her blue mantle symbolized eternity and human immortality. The cingulum (sash) was worn by young unmarried virgins, a symbol of chastity. The whiteness of the ermine fur showed Her purity; the eight-pointed stars on her mantle represented baptism and regeneration. To any European of the sixteenth century, the stars also represented the heavens, and Guadalupe's role as Queen of the Heavens.

But more importantly, Coatlaxopeuh was immediately recognizable to the Aztec, who were even more adept than Europeans at reading the language of images. Standing in front of the sun, Coatlaxopeuh was therefore greater than the sun god Huitzlipochtli. Her skin was the color of a native Mexica; Her blue-green mantle was the color once reserved for the divine couple of Aztec myth—Ometecuhtli and Omecihuatl; the white fur at Her neck and sleeves and the gold border were marks of royalty for the Aztecs; the broach at Her throat bore the same black cross carried by Cortés and the Spanish Friars; the sash at Coatlaxopeuh's waist was worn by pregnant women in Aztec culture; the child She carried was clearly divine. Flowers represented for the Aztec the experience of the divine. The single four-petalled flower over her womb represented the *ollin,* the familiar Aztec glyph for the Fifth Age, i.e., the present era. The cross-shaped flowers on her garment were the *mamalhuaztli*, signifying new life.

Much has been made of the seemingly supernatural, or at least inexplicable, qualities of the tilma image—the method by which the image is imprinted into the fibers; the reflection of the Bishop's image in the eye of the Virgin; the survival of the image after an anarchist exploded a bomb next to it in 1921—but there are *natural* features that prove equally stunning. Depicted on the Virgin's cloak is an accurate star map for 10:30 AM local time on the day that the image appeared on Juan Diego's tilma. Spain was in 1531 still using the Julian calendar, so the winter solstice took place on Tuesday, December 12. The main constellations of the northern sky are laid out on the right of the mantle; on the left are shown the southern constellations that can be seen from Tepeyac Hill in winter at dawn. (In the Aztec style, East is at the top of the map.)

The image is even dated according to Aztec practice—the three stars near the Virgin's foot represent the Aztec date of 13 Acatl, or 1531. Other groups of stars are placed not by their position in the sky, but to convey apocalyptic messages: the Corona Boreans (Boreal Crown) rests upon the Virgin's head; Virgo, the Virgin, is on her chest near her hands; Leo is on Her womb (she carries the Lion of Judah), with its main star Regulus, "the little king;" Gemini, the twins, are in the region of the knees; Orion, the Hunter, is over the angel.

America has long hunted for God, but it has been at times a monstrously errant hunt. Before the Spanish conquest, Tepeyac Hill was the site of a sacrificial pyramid dedicated to the Aztec lunar goddess Tonantzin, who was variously referred to as "Little Mother" (the patron of childbirth), "Goddess of Sustenance," and "Honored Grandmother." No doubt in some uncorrupted pre-Aztec form, Tonantzin had been a sustaining, nurturing, loving being, but in the hands of the post-Tlacaellel Aztec priests, she was a devouring, vengeful Spider goddess who ate her own children. Her fate was that of Huitzilopochtli and Tezcatlipoca, turned upside down by black magicians in service of the adversaries of the Sun Spirit.

Within weeks after she appeared to Juan Diego, Bishop Zamarraga ordered a shrine to be built where the Virgin had appeared. He entrusted the cloak with its miraculous image to Juan Diego, who moved into a small hermitage near the spot where the Virgin Mary had appeared, and he cared for the chapel and the first pilgrims who came to pray there, until his death in 1548. Even a decade before Juan Diego's death, only seven years after Coatlaxopeuh's appearance, 8 million Mexican natives were converted to the Catholic faith. Before the incident at Tepeyac Hill, the Franciscan and Dominican friars had been notoriously unsuccessful in their evangelization. Rebellions racked the countryside, and in the farther reaches of the old Aztec empire, heart sacrifice persisted. If one lets one's counterfactual imagination wander, it is possible to see Champlain and Hudson arriving upon the New World's shores, met there by native peoples in long-distance subjugation to an imperial capital to which they supply tribute and captives for massive, mechanical rituals of blood sacrifice. Cortes was extraordinarily lucky, arriving from the East in a One Reed year, resembling with his beard and black Good Friday garments the prophesied returning Quetzalcoatl. Champlain and Hudson—and those who followed— might not have been so fortunate.

6

COSMIC
COMMEMORATIONS

THE SUNDAY *Times* carried Mr. Joseph Ignatius Constantine Clarke's "Ode for the Hudson-Fulton Celebration," which opened:

Here at thy broad sea gate
On the ultimate ocean wave,
Where millions in hope have entered in,
Joyous, elate,
A home and a hearth to win;
For the promise you held and the bounty you gave,
Thou, and none other,
I call to thee, spirit; I call to thee, Mother,
America

Though there were plenty of papier-mâché goddesses on the parade floats; and official stationery and medallions bore the female Spirits of Progress, Commerce, History, Steam Navigation, and the Hudson River; and Lady Liberty silently oversaw the whole extravaganza from her perch in New York Harbor, the distaff side of America was poorly represented at the Hudson-Fulton events. Of the nearly one thousand members of the Commission, only a single one—a Mrs. Anson P. Atterbury—was a woman. No women attended the official banquet at the Hotel Astor. All of the Commission's committees had male secretaries. At the speeches, no women sat in the official boxes. If you search the photographs of the festivities, you must first squint a bit, and then from out of the male crowd emerges the occasional corseted, bonneted woman.

Rudolf Steiner spoke often of goddesses throughout his lecturing career. He was well acquainted with the mysteries of Gaea, Rhea, Hera, Athena, Demeter, Artemis, Natura, Nertheus, Thetis, Freya, Iblis, Ceridwen, Ishtar, and Isis. At the end of April 1909, Steiner gave a remarkable lecture entitled "Isis and Madonna." He began by speaking of how Goethe was inspired to send Faust to "the Mothers" after he read the Roman writer Plutarch's story of a man in Sicily who encounters these goddesses. He then turned his attention to Raphael's Sistine Chapel Madonna, and Michelangelo's *Piéta*, quoting Michelangelo as insisting that the youthfulness of the Virgin in his sculpture was faithful to reality, for it was universal knowledge that virgins preserve their youth. "We might go very far back," Steiner said, "and actually we should find the Madonna [portrayed in this way] all over the world. We might go to old India and there find the Goddess with the Krishna child at her breast; in a Chinese cult we might find similar pictures." He went on to discuss the Egyptian goddess Isis, in whom Steiner said one was given an ancient clairvoyant picture of the human soul, and that the Madonna was the modern image of the soul's "fructification out of the spirit": "In the Madonna we meet, as it were, with Isis reborn and in an appropriate way enhanced, transfigured."

A few weeks later, as he unfolded the pictures contained in the esoteric *Apocalypse* of John, Steiner spoke of Chapter 12's image of the woman clothed with the Sun, the Moon at her feet, and Her struggle with the Beast. Though he named the Beast—Sorath—he gave no name to the Woman. In early April, he had been in Malsch, Germany, to give an address on the occasion of the dedication of the Francis of Assisi branch of the Theosophical Society. Steiner had in 1907 in Munich for the Theosophical Congress designed a set of seven seals—whose motifs were related to each other in metamorphic series—to serve as sculpted capital reliefs on a set of columns. A young artist who attended the Congress asked Steiner what a building would look like that had such columns; Steiner described the space, and the young man set out to build a small model of the building in his hometown of Malsch, Germany. Steiner spoke these words as he laid the foundation stone for the building:

With the laying of this foundation stone of the Malsch building we entreat the blessings of the Masters of Wisdom and all
high and highest beings of the spiritual hierarchies that are
connected with earth evolution. We entreat that all of your
power of spirit may stream through in harmony all that is
brought, felt, willed, and done here. On this building may
there shine the light of the Spirits of the East; the Spirits of the
West may they reflect this light; the Spirits of the North may
they strengthen and the Spirits of the South warm it. So that
the Spirits of the East, West, North, and South may stream
through this building. In pain and suffering our Mother Earth
has become materialized. It is our task to once again spiritual-
ize her, to redeem her, in that through the power of our hands
we fashion a spirit-filled work of art. May this stone be a first
foundation stone for the redemption and transformation of
our planet Earth, and may the power of this stone work a
thousandfold.

The surprisingly modern expression "Mother Earth" was indeed
Steiner's, one that he used frequently. The deed of white magic he
performed at Malsch was both inspired by and preparatory for "the
Mother." The dedication ceremony was performed under a Full
Moon, as Rudolf Steiner was mindful that each Full Moon "remem-
bered" the moment of Christ's crucifixion, activating the forces of
Christ's etheric body and making them available for those who were
receptive.

This was Steiner's first attempt to build an "organic" temple or
cathedral dedicated to the spiritualization of Mother Earth. Four
years later—on a hill in Dornach, outside of Basel, Switzerland—he
would lay the foundation stone of the Goetheanum, a massive
expansion of the revolutionary temple that he had designed at
Malsch. As World War I ravaged Europe, a cadre of volunteers from
different nations—including those at war with each other—worked
to build a Grail temple to receive the Etheric Christ. The final stage
of Christ's descent into the Earth's etheric sphere began on June 15,
1920; on September 26th, the Goetheanum's opening ceremony was
held. The building, made almost entirely of wood, consisted of two

interpenetrating "rotundas"—really dodecahedrons, expressing the union of spirit and matter—of unequal diameter. Inside, the unusual forms in carved wood and reinforced concrete, watercolor murals, and engraved colored-glass windows were all illustrations of Steiner's anthroposophical principles.

In the new lecture hall of the Goetheanum a few months later, on Christmas Eve, Steiner took up the theme of Isis once again:

> Just as the Egyptians looked from Isis to Osiris, so we must learn to look again to the new Isis, the holy Sophia. The Christ will appear in spiritual form during the 20th century, not through an external happening, but inasmuch as human beings find that force which is represented by the holy Sophia. The present age has the tendency to lose this Isis-force, this force of the Mary. It was killed by all that arose with the modern consciousness of mankind. New forms of religion have in part exterminated just this view of the Mary.

This is the Mystery of modern humanity. The Mary-Isis has been killed, and she must be sought, just as Osiris was sought by Isis; but she must be sought in the wide space of heaven, with that force that Christ can awaken in us, if we give ourselves to Him in the right way.

Here, Steiner finally spoke openly of "Sophia," the goddess whose name he had spoken in so many of its other manifestations. The Goetheanum, a twentieth century Temple of Solomon, was itself a manifestation of Sophia as Wisdom, from which Steiner intended there to flow out to humanity streams of wisdom illuminating nature, history and the human being.

One of Sophia's most ancient contributions to humanity had been star wisdom, which like Isis-Mary-Sophia, had long ago been "killed." For two decades, Rudolf Steiner had not only been resurrecting the ancient star wisdom to teach it; he had been *living* it. Unnoticed by almost all of his students and colleagues, Steiner's daily activities—especially any that had a social, ritual element, like ceremonial occasions—frequently were attuned to starry configurations. In 1911 he had hinted at how this was true of Christ during his ministry, between the baptism in the Jordan and the Resurrection:

During the time that Jesus of Nazareth pursued his ministry and journeys as Jesus Christ in Palestine in the last three years of his life —from the age of thirty to thirty-three—the entire cosmic Christ-being continued to work in him. In other words, Christ always stood under the influence of the entire cosmos; he did not take a single step without cosmic forces working in him. The events of these three years in Jesus' life were a continuous realization of his horoscope, for in every moment during those years there occurred what usually happens only at birth ... the forces working in him were the cosmic forces coming from the sun and the stars; they directed his body. The total essence of the cosmos, to which the earth belongs, determined what Christ Jesus did.

Chapter 12 of John's *Apocalypse*, giving the image of the woman clothed with the Sun, the Moon under her feet, says that she had "a crown of twelve stars upon her head." This was an image of the entire zodiac, the "twelve stars" representing the twelve zodiacal constellations, which themselves stood for the entire starry heavens. The Virgin of Guadalupe—clearly a manifestation of Isis-Mary-Sophia—had both borne the stars upon her garment, and acted in accordance with the stars, in the timing of her apparition at the Feast of the Immaculate Conception. Given his role as the one to renew Sophia's ancient star wisdom, it was fitting that Rudolf Steiner's deeds would reflect this same acting in accordance with the stars. But Chapter 12 of John's *Apocalypse*, after speaking of Sophia's crown of stars, continues:

> And another portent appeared in heaven; behold a great dragon ... and the dragon stood before the woman who was about to bear a child, that he might devour her child when she brought it forth.

The heavenly woman pictured by John—Sophia, the Bride of the Lamb—had been with child for some time, quickening particularly in 1909, as her Bridegroom entered the sphere of the Archangels; but truly, with the founding of the temple of the new mysteries at Dornach, Sophia was giving birth, and as John had foreseen, the

Dragon meant to devour her child. Steiner's *Anthropos-Sophia*—the Sophianic wisdom *through* the human being—was born to prepare for the second coming of the Son, and in the process, was simultaneously manifesting the activity of the Mother.

On New Year's Eve in 1922 the Sun, at 16½° Sagittarius, stood opposite Pluto, at 16° Gemini in the sidereal zodiac. 16° Sagittarius marks the location of the Sun at the birth of Jesus; the return of the Sun to this position each year commemorates Jesus' birth in Bethlehem. Inwardly, Rudolf Steiner was fully aware of this, and planned the events of the day as a festival of commemoration of the divine birth. That evening, in the main hall of the Goetheanum, there was a eurythmy (an art of movement developed by Steiner) performance of the "Prologue in Heaven" of Goethe's *Faust,* followed by a lecture by Rudolf Steiner that spoke of how at the present time humanity was meant to enter into communion with the spiritual beings of the stars. Steiner closed the lecture with a meditation, to help lead his audience into the spiritual temple above, at the moment when the Etheric Christ was descending toward the temple of the earth.

Less than an hour before Steiner spoke the closing words of the meditation, it was discovered that a fire had broken out in the basement. The fire had already grown too large to extinguish, and at midnight, as the bells rang out the New Year, the temple of Anthropos—Sophia erupted in flame. The next morning, Rudolf Steiner stood amidst the ashes and announced that they would begin that day to rebuild Sophia's temple. A month after the fire, he gave a formula for understanding the parallel evolution of Sophia and humanity: like a human being, Sophia passes through evolutionary stages in the stream of historical time, but for Her the human biographical rhythm of 7-year periods becomes a rhythm of 7 to 800 years. "Thus we see a being weaving its way through history," Steiner said, "for whom a century is as one year. And . . . if we wished to, . . . we could write the biography . . . of this [being], who as regards spirituality is man's superior to the extent that a century is longer than a year." In a sense, the twentieth century marked the 21st year in the life of both humanity (20 centuries after the birth of Christ) and Sophia. Just as human individuals cross a critical threshold at age 21, with the full awakening of their Ego, Sophia's Ego at the threshold of the 21st century, lights up in mankind. The twentieth century marked a coming of age for both, and this threshold of adulthood meant that the dark powers would have a new plane of activity.

Though recently demoted as a planet, Pluto has a powerful effect on human beings. In its higher aspect Pluto is an expression of Phanes, which the Greek initiate Orpheus described as the source of the primal will underlying creation. Aligned with the higher aspect of Pluto, Rudolf Steiner had been enacting the divine will in the New Year's Eve commemoration of Jesus' birth. At Rudolf Steiner's own birth, Mars and Pluto were conjunct in sidereal Aries, whose main star Hamal is 56 times brighter than the Sun. Called in ancient times the "Messenger of Light," Hamal was associated in ancient Greece with Athena, the Goddess of Wisdom, i.e., it was believed to exert a powerful influence on human thinking capacity. Acting in its higher aspect, Pluto's conjunction with Hamal at the time of Steiner's birth was a sign of the remarkable intellectual gifts he would develop.

In its lower aspect Pluto expresses Hades, the god of the underworld, associated with the darker aspect of the will—the will to power. In the wake of Pluto's discovery (each of the three outer planet's discoveries marked important developments in human history) Adolf Hitler's will to power was exerted with full force, and part of the response to that force was the development of the atomic bomb—whose destructive violence gives an external picture of Pluto-Hades' influence within the human being. Pluto—Hades, in opposition to the Sun, was able to work its dark will upon Rudolf Steiner, the Goetheanum Grail temple, and humanity, because of the unconsciousness of the community who surrounded Steiner.

Pluto played a role in an even more devastating eruption of unconsciousness 10 years later. On January 11, 1933, the Sun—at 27° Sagittarius—was in opposition to Pluto—at 28° Gemini—once again. In addition, there was a Full Moon—at 27° Gemini. This was an extraordinarily important Full Moon, for it was the first Full Moon after the completion of Christ's descent to the Earth's etheric realm. Since the crucifixion took place at the time of the Full Moon,

it is fitting to think of this January 11, 1933 Full Moon as the beginning of the "New Age," a marker as significant for our time as the
date of Jesus' birth was two thousand years ago. Just two and a half
weeks after this Full Moon in conjunction with Pluto, Adolf Hitler
became Reichschancellor of Germany, declaring that a new, glorious, eternal age—the Third Reich—had begun.

At the greatest moments of cosmic commemoration playing
down into human history, Evil strikes. The Beast, having no creative
powers of his own, usurps the great rhythms emanating from the
spiritual beings of the cosmos, and misses no opportunity to offer to
humanity over and over again counterfeit, caricatured forms of its
own true destiny. In January 1933, at the moment of the Etheric
Christ's birth, and of Sophia and humanity's 21st birthday, an
imposter child was substituted, but no one at the party took notice.

John had taken notice 2000 years before, catching in his visions
in the cave on Patmos a glimpse of this future event: "'Woe to you,
O earth and sea, for the devil has come down to you in great wrath,
because he knows that his time is short!' And when the dragon saw
that he had been thrown down to the earth, he pursued the woman
who had borne the male child." (*Revelation* 12:12–13) And Rudolf
Steiner had taken notice and spoken of it in 1909, when he revealed
the nature of Sorath, a decade before the Beast, employing Pluto/
Hades' fiery emanations, had pursued *him*. Indeed, Rudolf Steiner
had spoken about the direct relationship existing between the mystery of death and the mystery of evil, a relationship that comes into
focus in the twentieth century:

> Today, when Christ is to appear again—though now in an
> etheric form—when a kind of Mystery of Golgotha is to be
> experienced anew, evil will have a significance similar to that
> which birth and death had for the fourth post-Atlantean epoch
> [i.e., the Greco-roman era, 747 BC to AD 1414].... Thus by a
> strange paradox mankind will in the fifth post-Atlantean epoch
> be led through the forces of evil to the renewal of the Mystery of
> Golgotha. Through the experience of evil it will be possible for
> the Christ to appear again, just as He appeared in the fourth
> post-Atlantean epoch through the experience of death.

History is *always* silently marking innumerable commemorations, but the twentieth century saw the conjunction of some stupendous ones. January 11, 1933 marked the exact completion of 57 cycles of 33⅓ years since the Mystery of Golgotha; two weeks later Adolf Hitler came to power. Two more "Christ rhythms" brought the completion of the 59th cycle on September 8, 1999, bringing the 33-year Christ rhythm into close alignment with the third cycle of Sorath's number—1998.

Spuyten Duyvil, September, 1909

While in the Champlain Valley there had been a great dispute over the proper location for a monument to Samuel de Champlain, in the expectedly more contentious terrain of Manhattan, all were agreed that a monument to Henry Hudson would have to go on Spuyten Duyvil Hill. The hill overlooked both the Spuyten Duyvil Creek—the northern boundary of Manhattan Island—and the spot where the *Half Moon*, at anchor on *Mahicanituk*, was attacked by Lenape men in canoes from *Nipinechsen*, the village at the mouth of the creek. Hudson's first mate John Juet's account had captured the imagination of generations of New York City historians. Juet's journal entry of September 4, 1609 described the first meeting with "the people of the country" when they came aboard the *Half Moon*. The natives:

> Seem[ed] very glad of our coming, and brought green tobacco, and gave us of it for knives and beads. They go in deerskins loose, well dressed. They have yellow copper. They desire clothes, and are very civil.

Hudson and his men were not so civil; they kidnapped a couple of the *Nipinechsen* men who had come aboard to trade, and continued on upriver, still searching for the Northwest Passage. On October 2nd, as the ship was returning downriver, and lay with its head downstream, waiting for the tide to turn, two canoes full of Indians shot arrows at them from the stern. After shooting two or three of these men, the *Half Moon* pulled up anchor and floated down river on the ebb tide. At the spot that today is Fort Washington Point

(Bennett Park, between West 183rd and West 185th Sts.), about a hundred more men from *Nipinechsen* appeared alongshore and harassed them.

> There I shot a falcon [gun] at them, and killed two of them, whereupon the rest fled into the woods. Yet they manned off another canoe with nine or ten men, which came to meet us; so I shot at it also a falcon, and shot it through, and killed one of them. Then our men with their muskets killed three or four more of them. So they went their way. Within a while after, we got down two leagues beyond that place and anchored in a bay clear from all danger of them on the other side of the river ... [the side] called Manna-hata. There we saw no people to trouble us, and rode quietly all night, but had much wind and rain.

There was no other account of the September 1609 encounter, but Juet's brief entries were enough to provide anyone who read them with the necessary skeleton for a vivid story. Juet's account was in the mind of Spuyten Duyvil Hill resident William Muschenheim, proprietor of the Hotel Astor, who for years had dug up hundreds of stone objects and pottery from his garden on land nearby. Muschenheim was the one who first proposed and then lobbied for the idea of the monument. Since the elevation of Spuyten Duyvil Hill was 200 feet, the notion arose that this by lucky coincidence denoted the number of years between Hudson's arrival and the invention of steam navigation; by erecting a 100-foot tall granite obelisk the planners would set Hudson's statue at an elevation suggesting the Tercentenary of Hudson's advent. At the base of the monument there is a bronze relief showing Hudson offering a handful of glass beads to a kneeling Lenape man.

On September 27, a ceremony was held for the laying of the cornerstone of the monument, attended by a group of "real Iroquois Indians"—though the village here had been Lenape. While the great international war fleet—along with the replica *Half Moon* and *Clermont*—lay at anchor in the river, a procession of a half dozen speakers trumpeted the solemn historicity of the occasion. During his speech, Governor Charles Hughes paused to mourn the cruel fate of Hudson, who had on a subsequent voyage to search for the Northwest Passage, been set adrift in a small boat among the ice floes by his mutinous crew.

The monument committee had brought along a time capsule—a steel box—to be placed under the cornerstone, and during the ceremony, the items were announced and then placed into the box: the official publications of the Hudson-Fulton Commission; a collection of photographs of the site and views from there; a set of the commemorative medallions; a copy of each of the city's morning newspapers, and one of the afternoon editions. The *New York Times* front page predictably focused on the Celebration:

HOTELS PACKED, STREETS FILLED FOR FETE WEEK

Late Visitors to the Great Celebration Finding It
Hard to Get a Lodging

FLEET TO ILLUMINATE AGAIN

A Repetition of the Beautiful Spectacle Decided
on for Next Saturday

PEARY'S SHIP IN THE PARADE

Roosevelt Coming from Maine and Will Be Seen with the
Explorer in Command

TO-DAY IS DEDICATION DAY

Hudson Monument at Spuyten Duyvil to be Unveiled to Saluting Guns—Interstate Park Opened, Too

A side column headline gave evidence of the less glamorous side of the gathering, reporting on accidents caused by the throngs of automobiles crowding to see the naval parade:

TWO CHILDREN DIE UNDER AUTO WHEELS

Avoiding Boy in Street, Chauffeur Runs Upon Sidewalk,
Crushing 2-Year-Old Girl

TAXICAB KILLS BOY OF 7

Witnesses Say He Ran Before It—A Number of Minor Automobile Accidents During the Day

The real news however was the latest report on the feud between the polar explorers Robert Peary and Frederick Cook:

PEARY'S ACCOUNT OF IT

Wanted No Cook Supplies Aboard—Doesn't Believe Cook Left Instruments

DR. COOK TROUBLED

ARCTIC BOX MISSING

It seems that leaving a box for posterity didn't always guarantee that posterity—or even the next explorer to come along—would find it. Peary, who had just returned from his North Pole expedition, was skeptical that Cook had reached the pole the year before, as he claimed he had done. Historians today doubt that either of them actually made it to the geographical pole. Three hundred years after Hudson and Champlain, exploration and discovery was still a tricky business.

7

2009: PERIGEE

ANOTHER HEADLINE on the front page of the time capsule's copy of the *Times* announced that President William Howard Taft, on a presidential tour through Salt Lake City, had given the sermon the day before at the Mormon Tabernacle, making an appeal for "fairness and amity:"

AMERICANS ARE TOO CURT

Life Isn't Made Up of Grandstand Plays, He Asserts

After the sermon Taft was chauffeured to Ogden to review a gathering of 20,000 Mormon schoolchildren. At one point in the line, more than a thousand children were dressed in red, white, and blue caps and capes, and arranged in the form of an American flag.

In the back pages of the *Times* were the little notices for Sunday services at Manhattan's churches—including the new-fangled churches like Christian Science and Theosophy. At that time, even before Rudolf Steiner's formal split with the Theosophical Society over the Krishnamurti affair, there were a group of individuals meeting regularly in New York City who were intensively studying the work of Rudolf Steiner. The "Saint Mark Group" met in the Carnegie Hall studio of Herbert Wilber Greene, president of the National Singing Teachers Association, and associate editor of *Étude* magazine. The group's members were aspiring instrumentalists, singers, and artists, many of them current or former students of Greene's.

In 1909, the group would probably have been studying Rudolf Steiner's latest work, just published in New York, *Initiation and Its Results*. They would not have known that on September 26, Steiner had given the last lecture in a series of ten devoted to the Gospel of

St. Luke. In the penultimate chapter of that lecture, Steiner says:

> More than any other document, the Luke Gospel, if fully understood, fills human souls with the warm love that allows peace to dwell on earth as the most exquisite reflection of divine mysteries. Revelations must be reflected on earth, reflected back into the spiritual heights. If we acknowledge spiritual science in this sense, it will reveal the mysteries of divine spiritual beings and spiritual existence, and the reflection of these revelations will dwell in our souls as love and peace, the most exquisite earthly reflection of what streams down to us from the heights.

"Revelations must be reflected on earth, reflected back into the spiritual heights"; after he began his career as spiritual teacher in 1900, Rudolf Steiner enacted this service every day of his life. His life and teachings—nowhere yet was this more true than in these ten lectures on Luke—were a spectacular example of the great truth that there is no end to revelation, and that working consciously with sublime spiritual truths is a deed of service to the spiritual world as well as to humanity.

By 1925, the year that Rudolf Steiner died, there were no more than about a hundred anthroposophists in the entire United States, but the greatest concentration could still be found in Manhattan, in the neighborhood of Sixth Avenue and Fifty-Sixth Street. Led by *Herald-Tribune* journalist Ralph Courtney, they opened the Threefold Vegetarian Restaurant in 1924; patrons could choose from items like the daily vegetable plate (40¢); vegetable casserole (20¢); and for dessert, cranberry sundae (15¢). Because the predominantly female clientele could not persuade their boyfriends and husbands to frequent a place with solely vegetarian fare, a daily meat dish was eventually offered. Patrons uninitiated into the esoteric world of anthroposophy received a gentle introduction: the small grocery store in front of the restaurant sold homeopathic herbal remedies and pharmaceuticals; distinctive anthroposophical artwork graced the walls; the wooden chairs and tables—their curved designs reflecting the cosmic formative forces—were sculpted out of the same principles Steiner had used to design the Goetheanum.

In 1926 a group of the Manhattan anthroposophists, looking for a rural place to extend their efforts at social, cultural, and ecological renewal, bought a farm in Spring Valley, New York. By 1933 the Threefold Farm was holding annual summer conferences, and in 1942, a former pupil of Rudolf Steiner, Ehrenfried Pfeiffer, came to live at the farm, establishing a laboratory where he pioneered methods of sensitive crystallization and biodynamic agriculture.

In the following decades, students of Rudolf Steiner kept spreading north up the Hudson Valley. The Anthroposophic Press, which continued to bring out editions of Steiner's lectures, moved from New York City up to Hudson, New York in 1982. (In October 1909, during the Hudson-Fulton celebration, the village of Hudson had received the *Half Moon* on its riverfront, and the local chapter of the Daughters of the American Revolution had presented the town with a large fountain surmounted by a pair of bronze medallions depicting Hudson and Fulton.) In 1996, the Anthroposophic Press published *Chronicle of the Living Christ: The Life and Ministry of Jesus Christ: Foundations of Cosmic Christianity*, by Robert Powell. A former lecturer in mathematics and statistics at Brighton Polytechnic in England, Powell had left in 1976 to study and lecture in astronomy and the history of astronomy, and then gone on to study eurythmy, an art of movement developed by Rudolf Steiner.

On the opening page of *Chronicle of the Living Christ* appeared the provocative statement made by Rudolf Steiner in 1911, that every step taken by Christ during his ministry was in harmony with—and an expression of—the entire cosmos. Taking this single statement as his inspiration, Powell set out to exactly identify the chronology of Christ's ministry, from the baptism in the Jordan until the crucifixion. Despite the fact that Christianity rests squarely on historical events—the life, death, and resurrection of Jesus Christ—the actual dates of Christ's birth and death were never transmitted. The four gospels—the historical record of Jesus' life—do not mention any explicit dates. To this day, scholars disagree about the timing of all the important dates in Jesus Christ's life.

Powell worked both from his knowledge of astronomy, and from the indications of Rudolf Steiner and Anne Catherine Emmerich, a German woman who, between 1820 and 1824, communicated visions of the day-to-day life of Jesus, including the period of Christ's ministry. Emmerich described in incredible detail the places Christ visited, the miracles and healings he performed, his teaching activity, and the people with whom he interacted. Here for example, is her description of the building owned by Joseph of Arimathea, where the Last Supper took place:

> On the southern side of Mount Sion, not far from the ruined Castle of David, and the market held on the ascent leading to that Castle, there stood, towards the east, an ancient and solid building, between rows of thick trees, in the midst of a spacious court surrounded by strong walls. To the right and left of the entrance, other buildings were to be seen adjoining the wall, particularly to the right, where stood the dwelling of the major-domo. . . . I saw Nicodemus in the buildings to the left of the court, where a great many stones which filled up the passages leading to the supper-room had been placed. A week before, I had seen several persons engaged in putting the stones on one side, cleaning the court, and preparing the supper-room for the celebration of the Pasch.

Anne Catherine's eyewitness account gave Powell important details for corroborating his chronology, allowing him to precisely determine Jesus' date of birth (around midnight on December 6, 2 BC), the date of the baptism (September 23, AD 29) and resurrection (April 5, AD 33).

Rudolf Steiner had spoken of the resurrection as the birth of the Risen Christ, and pointed to the importance of the 33-year rhythm in the life of Jesus Christ leading up to that birth. But for a clock as exquisitely timed as the cosmos, one needs more exactitude than "33⅓." With the dates from Jesus' life firmly established, Robert Powell could now say that the exact length of Jesus' life from birth to the resurrection was 33⅓ years, minus 1½ days (i.e., 33.329 years). Powell plotted this rhythm through time until he landed in the twentieth century: 56 cycles of the Christ rhythm from April 5, AD 33, brought one to September 10, 1899; 57 cycles to January 8, 1933; 58 cycles to May 9, 1966; and 59 cycles to September 6, 1999. He also transposed not just the end—resurrection—date, but the *entire* "calendar" of Christ's life after the baptism, creating a table that matched the dates to the present time: e.g., Friday, September 23, in the year 2 = Saturday, February 24, 1996; Saturday, September 24, AD 29 = Sunday, February 25, 1996, and so on, leading up to the last resurrection date (April 5, AD 33) to occur in the twentieth century, Monday, September 6, 1999. Paired with a descriptive chronicle drawn largely from Anne Catherine Emmerich's visions, the intention of this calendar was to provide a guide for *inner commemoration* of the day-to-day life of Christ's ministry, allowing one to experience inwardly something like Anne Catherine's communion.

Because Jesus' last 3⅓ years—the period of Christ's ministry—represented the most intense revelation, Robert Powell then went on to identify the corresponding periods in the twentieth century, along with attempting to understand both the nature of the divine impulse carried by the Christ rhythm, and the counter-impulse opposing the new revelation of the Etheric Christ. In the first period, from June 29, 1929 to January 8, 1933, Christ worked to inspire human beings to awake to the presence of the divine within themselves, and to free themselves from the ancient, regressive forces of blood and tribal/nation state affinity.

Even the most cursory assessment of twentieth century history shows that there was a spectacular eruption of these forces from 1929 to 1933, culminating in the *"Blut und Boden"* (Blood and Soil) slogan of the Nazis. The counter-image presented to the German people was a direct attack on the free individuality that Christ was seeking to inspire and support. The tremendous effect of Hitler's black magical movement came about through seizing the will element in the human being. Through the controlled activation of the will—via sporting events, mass gatherings, parades, and pseudo-sacred nocturnal open-air festivals like the Nuremberg Rallies—a consciousness-dimming fascination was aroused. We speak of the "enthusiasm" of the crowd; literally the word means the God within. But the feelings aroused by *Der Führer* were the opposite of nurturing the God within. The demon dwelling in Hitler was poured directly into the souls of all who looked up at him in admiration. Robert Powell recognized the uncanny symmetry with Christ's encounter with the temptation of the will to power in Matthew 4:9, where Satan promises Christ vast rewards "If you will fall down and worship me." Christ's response to Satan, "You shall worship the Lord your God and him only shall you serve," was totally forgotten by the German people, who succumbed *en masse* to the temptation of the will to power.

In the second period of Christ's intense working in the etheric, from October 27, 1962 to May 9, 1966, the impulse was meant to be an awakening to love and community—seen in America in the wave of intentional communities, the flourishing of the antiwar movement, the women's movement, and the triumph of the civil rights movement, this impulse found expression in the liberation movements in Latin America and Africa. Once again, however, the Christ impulse met opposition. From the dark machinations standing behind the assassinations of President John F. Kennedy, his brother Bobby, Martin Luther King, Jr., and other American leaders, to the destructive illusions fostered by the drug culture, a second temptation was afoot. Matthew (4:5) describes Satan's second temptation of Christ as "casting oneself down from the pinnacle of the Temple." Certainly the 1960s saw this in the hedonistic surrender to base instinctual urges, often with the help of the new intoxicant LSD—introduced to the world by the CIA. Instead of striving toward the pinnacle of the Temple—the clear light of conscience and reason—a generation cast itself down by abandoning ego consciousness in favor of subconscious drives and impulses.

At century's end, from February 24, 1996 to September 6, 1999, Christ, seeking to awaken humanity to the reality of the living substance of the Divine Mother—expressed in the global environmental movement—was met by opposition once more. The last temptation of Christ, described in Matthew 4:3 was "to turn stones into bread," manifested in the global explosion of *virtual* realities, ersatz digital copies of real life. The adversary's attack seems even more demonic in that it is directed at children, and thus at the future.

Along with this mapping onto the twentieth century of the rhythm of Christ's *etheric* body, Robert Powell uncovered the rhythm of Christ's *astral* body. This rhythm Powell found while researching the question of the duration of Christ's ministry. The prevailing theories among scholars were that the ministry lasted a little over one, two, or three years; Powell determined that the ministry lasted 3⅓ years—exactly 1290 days. With this knowledge in hand, combined with a study of the corresponding movements of the planets, Powell was able to chronicle on a daily basis for the 3⅓-year period, the relationship between Christ's activities and the activity of the planets against the backdrop of the zodiac. One of the first extraordinary discoveries made by Powell was that a single day in the period of Christ's ministry was equal to 29½ years (or more accurately, 29.4578 years) in human history. This is the orbital period of Saturn/Kronos, the venerable keeper of Time. As the guardian of cosmic memory, Saturn "inscribed" the events of Christ's ministry into Time, in such a way that the deeds of the ministry come to expression in human history. "In other words," stated Powell, "Christ lived out in advance, during the 1290 days of the ministry, the entire future course of the world in archetypal form. This means that the 'end of the world' will be the Mystery of Golgotha —death and resurrection—for the whole of humanity."

Powell's "Apocalypse Code"—so-called because this calculus can be correlated with the events described in John's *Apocalypse*—meant that he could determine that "end of the world" date to the year AD 38,033. i.e., (1290 x 29.4578) + 33. Powell's reckoning agrees almost exactly with the date given by Rudolf Steiner, who put the end of the 7th post-Atlantean period in AD 38,134. Given the imminence of most modern apocalyptic pronouncements, this date gives a generous amount of breathing room. But Powell recognized a more immediate challenge, based on events of a particular period in Christ's ministry. At the start of the Sabbath on the evening of Friday, October 21, AD 29, Jesus began his forty days in the wilderness, praying and fasting in a small cave on the slope of Mt. Attarus. During this forty-day period, Christ was subjected daily to temptation by Satan, but he resisted these temptations. On the afternoon of the last day of the fast—November 30, AD 29—Saturn stood exactly opposite the Sun, a cosmic sign of the victory over evil by the Father, through the Son. Using his "Apocalypse Code," Powell determined this date to be the year 2049.

Before Christ's victory over the Prince of Darkness, there had been an intensification of the temptations during the last three days in the wilderness, as seen above in the following of the 33⅓-year rhythm's last 3½-year periods in the twentieth century. On the last night of Christ's trials on Mt. Attarus, the Sun was conjunct Pluto at 9° Sagittarius. In historical terms, this translates to the year 2010. Since Saturn is the bearer of cosmic memory, every time Saturn reaches 9° Sagittarius the climax of the temptations in the wilderness is remembered, and thus cosmically activated. Powell also considered the critical role of the outer planets—Uranus, Neptune, and Pluto—finding them crossing 9° Sagittarius respectively in 1986, 1989, and 2010; he pointed in particular to the 2010 date, which recalls Pluto's actual position at the climax of the temptation in the wilderness.

∗

There are always cycles within cycles, and "remembrances" within remembrances. Around midday on November 24, AD 29, five days before the day of the last temptation, there was a total eclipse of the Sun at 4° Sagittarius, which signified for Jesus Christ *the opening of the gates of hell*, leading to his meeting with Satan.

There was a partial solar eclipse in June 1909, and the only reports in the newspapers were about the scientific disappointment at American observatories, since the weather across the nation was cloudy. The papers noted that Charles Peary and his crew, in search of the North Pole, would be able to see it though. Unlike reportage at the time of Mars' approach or the spectacle of Halley's Comet, pundits and philosophers did not seize upon the occasion to remind the public of how superstitious people of the past saw ill omen in solar eclipses.

One thoroughly modern Manhattanite, Charles Fort, was *very* superstitious—or at least suspicious—about eclipses. What had come to his attention from his New York Public Library research was that eclipses—both solar and lunar, partial and total—routinely were accompanied by some very odd occurrences. In Bruges, Belgium, in March 1848, instead of darkening at the moment of the total lunar eclipse, the moon shone blood red, illuminated "as perfect with light as if there had been no eclipse whatever." Antarctic explorer Robert Scott reported in his *Voyage of the Discovery* that on September 21, 1903, at the time of nine-tenths of totality, he had seen the sun shining brightly in an overcast sky.

And then there was also the fact that the earth, during daylight hours, had been overcome in many places at many different times by profound darkness—when no solar eclipse was meant to occur. In 1857 in Amsterdam, in the midst of a perfect halcyon day, darkness so intense and terrifying had descended, that "many panic-stricken persons lost their lives stumbling into the canals." London: August 19, 1763, a darkness "greater than at the great eclipse of 1748." Oshkosh, Wisconsin: March 19, 1886, at 3 PM, in five minutes the darkness equaled that of midnight. Memphis, Tennessee: 10 AM, Dec. 2, 1904, for about fifteen minutes, darkness so total that "in some quarters a panic prevailed . . . [some people] shouting and praying and imagining that the end of the world had come." Louisville, Kentucky: March 7, 1911, at about 8 AM: for about half an hour, the "intense blackness and generally ominous appearance of the storm spread terror throughout the city."

Fort was by no means surprised at the lack of scientific attention to these anomalous episodes. He realized that anyone who spoke would have:

> felt the blight of a Dominant; that Materialistic Science was a jealous god, excluding, as works of the devil, all utterances against the seemingly uniform, regular, periodic; that to defy him would have brought on—withering by ridicule—shrinking away by publishers—contempt of friends and family—justifiable grounds for divorce—that one who would so defy would feel what unbelievers in relics of saints felt in an earlier age; what befell virgins who forgot to keep the fires burning, in a still earlier age—but that, if he'd almost absolutely hold out, just the same—new fixed star reported in Monthly Notices.

Fort said he felt "pretty well-eclipsed" himself as to the actual explanation, but he knew much better than that. Passing on to storm clouds described as having fangs, and to sulphur-belching clouds coming out of nowhere, Fort hinted strongly that he scented something infernal about the whole business of eclipses, predicted and unpredicted: "In many instances, objects, or meteoritic stones, that have come from this earth's externality, have had a sulphurous odor. Why a wind effect should be sulphurous is not clear. That a vast object from external regions should be sulphurous is in line with many data."

Assessing all this "damned" data, Fort even put quotation marks around the word "objects," suggesting these were not inanimate but "super-biologic phenomena." All he could do was to put his case before his readers and leave it at that:

> Explain or express or accept, and what does it matter? Our attitude is:
> Here are the data.
> See for yourself.
> What does it matter what my notions may be?
> Here are the data.

But even with the intense contemporary interest in Fort, *no one*, particularly scientists, has taken hold of such data as Fort offered up. To make sense of eclipses, one must escape the "blight of the Dominant," the clutches of the "jealous god," Materialism. Rudolf Steiner had offered insight into the spiritual effects of eclipses; in September 1922, a few days after a total solar eclipse had passed over central Australia, he said:

> At the time of a solar eclipse ... something totally different takes place in the part of the earth affected from what is happening when there is no eclipse. When we know that on the one hand the rays of the sun penetrate down to the earth and on the other hand the forces or rays of will stream out to meet the sun, it is possible to form some idea of how a solar eclipse can affect these radiations of will which are altogether spiritual in their nature. The sunlight is blocked by the moon; that is a purely physical process. But physical matter—in this case the body of the moon—is no obstacle to the forces streaming out from the will. These forces radiate into the darkness, and there ensues a period of time, short though it may be, in which all that is of the nature of will upon the earth flows out into universal space in an abnormal way. It is different altogether from

what takes place when there is no eclipse. Ordinarily, the physical sunlight unites with the radiations of will streaming towards it. When there is an eclipse, the forces of will flow unhindered into cosmic space.

The old initiates knew these things. They saw that at such a moment all the unbridled impulses and instincts of humanity surge out into the cosmos. And they gave their pupils the following explanation. They said: Under normal conditions the evil impulses of will which are sent out into the cosmos by human beings are, as it were, burned up and consumed by the rays of the sun, so that they can injure only man himself, but can do no universal harm. When, however, there is an eclipse of the sun, opportunity is given for the evil which is willed on earth to spread over the cosmos. An eclipse is a physical event behind which there lies a significant spiritual reality. . . .

Eclipses of the sun and moon, recurring as they do in the course of every year, may really be looked upon as "safety-valves." A safety-valve is there to avert danger, to provide an outlet for something or other—steam, for instance—at the right moment. One of the safety-valves which makes its appearance in the cosmos and to which we give the name of a solar eclipse, serves the purpose of carrying out into space in a Luciferic way, the evil that spreads over the earth, in order that evil may work havoc in a wider, less concentrated sphere. . . .

Man will not be able to free himself from the forces in his being which tend to drag him downwards until he develops in himself a certain feeling for spiritual concepts such as these.

With his powers of clairvoyance, Rudolf Steiner clarified partially the mystery that unnerved Charles Fort: at a solar eclipse, negative aspects of existence are freed up. Though Steiner speaks of the human will, one can imagine that the will of spiritual beings—both good and evil—is also given liberty at the time of the eclipse. The "sulphurous" scent detected by Fort was his intuition of the real nature of his anomalous eclipse data. Fort never took up the Tunguska mystery in any of his books, but with Steiner's insight to guide us, and a Fortean sensitivity to "conjunctions" of planetary events, the fact that on June 28—two days before the Tunguska "explosion"—there was a total eclipse of the Sun, should arrest our attention. On the day between, June 29, less than 12 hours before the catastrophic event above the Siberian taiga forest, Rudolf Steiner had strenuously warned of the activity of the Sun Demon, Sorath.

There was at the time of the Tunguska event a massive solar flare, which seems to indicate a healing, protective response from the Sun Spirit. Such activity is the *real* "Star Wars," and as in George Lucas's fictional myth, human beings are on the front lines of this galactic battle. Rudolf Steiner's remarks make it clear that the eclipse of the Sun's forces is an occasion for human beings to call forth their own *inner* Sun forces, giving gratitude for the Sun not just as a source of light and warmth, but as the dwelling place of majestic spiritual beings—particularly, the home of the Sun Spirit, Christ.

Next summer, on July 22, 2009—just two weeks after the Champlain Valley will celebrate the 400th birthday of "History" in the region, and two months before Manhattan and the Hudson Valley will do the same—there will be a total eclipse of the Sun at 2:36 AM Greenwich Mean Time. The path of the eclipse will cross India, Nepal, Bangladesh, Bhutan, China, the southern islands of Japan, and the western Pacific Ocean. The Moon will be at its perigee (its closest position to the Earth), making it larger than the Sun, resulting in a wider path and greater duration. (The arc of the partial eclipse will swing as far north as 60° N, right across northern Russia, and as far south as 30° S, touching the North Island of New Zealand) These are conditions that will allow for the maximum power of evil to penetrate toward the Earth, should human beings remain unaware of their own participation in this event.

When Sorath violently burst into the earth's atmosphere at the end of June, 1908, just before the advent of the Etheric Christ in the sphere of the Archangels, there was a spectacular "bunching" of planets. Along with the near conjunction of the Sun (at 14° Gemini), Mercury (22° Gemini), the Moon (26° Gemini), and Venus (21° Gemini), Uranus (at 22° Sagittarius) was in opposition with Mercury, Moon, and Mars (at 1° Cancer). Saturn (18° Pisces) was square Mercury & Moon. Pluto was also in Gemini, at 1°. Vast cosmic forces—available for the activity of both the Sun Spirit and the Sun Demon—were in resonance on June 30, 1908, but *there was no assistance from human beings, since they were oblivious to the event.*

At the time of the July 22, 2009 eclipse, there will be a triple conjunction of Jupiter, Neptune, and Chiron (formerly called an asteroid, it is now classified as a "centaur," suggesting its nature as half comet, half asteroid)—all within less than a single degree, and also a heliocentric opposition of Saturn with Uranus. No doomsday events have been forecast for that date; eclipses long ago lost their power to frighten mankind. Indeed, dozens of eclipse-watching tours to China and the South Pacific are already sold out. Sirius Travel's 11-day China tour ($3,850) will take in the eclipse from Emei Shan, a sacred mountain in central China; advertisements for *Sky & Telescope Magazine's* "South Pacific" tour boast: "With so few cruise ships available for this eclipse, and only 160 staterooms on the elegant *Paul Gauguin*, this eclipse voyage is sure to sell out"; for $3,499, "Ring of Fire" expeditions will take eclipse watchers out to Iwo Jima island for five minutes and twelve seconds of totality.

Eclipse tourism does not change the fact that at the time of a total solar eclipse, as Charles Fort so presciently pointed out, something sulphurous is stirred up. Fort only hinted at *who* this might be; Rudolf Steiner was much more explicit: "Evil thoughts from cosmic space can come to those human beings who quite especially want to be possessed by evil thoughts." Not only are demonic spiritual beings agitated at the time of an eclipse, but they can be taken hold of at that time by black magicians. Very few people are able to discern this working of evil at the time of a solar eclipse.

At 2 AM on February 5, 1962, amidst a rare "stellium" (cluster) of the seven classical planets (plus Chiron) in the sign of Capricorn, there was a total eclipse of the sun whose path of totality passed over Indonesia, New Guinea, and the eastern Pacific Ocean. At 7:17 AM, as she readied herself to greet the rising sun by reciting the 23rd Psalm, American psychic Jeane Dixon instead beheld this picture:

> The bare-limb trees of the city had given way to an endless desert scene, broiled by a relentless sun. Glowing like an enormous ball of fire, the sun had cracked the horizon, emitting

brilliant rays of scintillating light, which seemed to attract the earth like a magic wand. The sun's rays parted, facilitating the appearance of the Egyptian Pharaoh Akhenaten and Queen Nefertiti. But my eyes were drawn to the new-born-child she tenderly cradled in her other arm. He was wrapped in soiled, ragged swaddling clothes, in stark contrast to the magnificently arrayed royal couple. I then became aware of a multitude of people that appeared. I witnessed Nefertiti hand the child to the people. Instantly rays of sunlight burst forth from the little boy, which blended with the brilliance of the sun. My eyes once more focused on the baby. By now he had grown to manhood, and a small cross, which had formed above his head enlarged and expanded until it covered the earth in all directions. Suffering people, of all races, knelt in worshipful adoration, lifting their arms and offering their hearts to him.

Jeane Dixon—whose elegant Washington, D.C. townhouse was less than a mile from the White House—looked over at her bedside clock to see the time, and then recorded her waking vision. Her first impression was that she had witnessed the birth of a great king who would revolutionize the world. At the end of her vision, however, she saw that while most people followed the man, a small group followed a narrow path away from him. By 1969, when she published *My Life and Prophecies*, the "Washington Seeress" had concluded that the man in the flowing robe was the Antichrist, who would "form a new all-embracing doctrine based on his almighty power."

Though the February 1962 vision was of a child born in the Middle East, Dixon had other visions connecting this individual to America:

> I have seen a "government within a government" develop in the United States within the last few years. . . . I see this "government within a government" being controlled and financed by a well-oiled political "machine" of one of our leading political families. With their eye on the White House, I see them discredit any man who occupies it without their approval, no matter how good his political programs may be.

They will—through political intimidation, propaganda, and illegal sixth-column activities—make every effort to show the nation that only their man, the one who heads their "machine," has the sole right to occupy the White House. Their campaign is going to cause great harm to our nation both here and abroad.

I "see" this group succeed in taking over de facto control of the country. They will give rise to an upheaval in our social structure as never before seen. They will bring about increased social unrest and great discontent. Foreign subversive elements will—as they did in the 1960s—infiltrate the unruly factions and cause renewed fighting on the nation's campuses and in racial ghettos.

All of the evil in the masses will be swept toward an unknown frenzy by this "machine". . . .

The daughter of a wealthy Wisconsin lumber baron, Dixon had married a successful businessman who after World War II had become a D.C. real estate tycoon; she served as secretary/treasurer and later CEO of the realty company. As a Washington socialite who frequented diplomatic functions and parties at the homes of capitol city power brokers, Jeane Dixon was a member of the D.C. establishment. A devout Catholic, her politics were right-wing Republican; she maintained close friendships with FBI director J. Edgar Hoover, Senator Strom Thurmond, and President Ronald Reagan and his wife Nancy. The book that recounts her 1962 vision is filled with bitter polemics against civil rights and anti-war activists, whom she believed were unwitting tools of Soviet agents. Dixon's fervent patriotism makes her declaration of a dark governmental conspiracy with the Antichrist all the more striking:

His disciples . . . will have the power and the propaganda machine of the United States backing them, advancing his cause beyond anything ever thought possible.

Like Christ, the Antichrist will center his work at the city of Jerusalem. I get the distinct feeling that the religions of the world will somehow merge with the philosophies of the East. I see the youth flock to him and partake of his wisdom.

As a devoted Bible student, Jeane Dixon interpreted her visions through the lens of John's *Revelations*, Chapter 13:

> And I beheld another beast coming up out of the earth; and he had two horns like a lamb, and he spake as a dragon. And he exerciseth all the power of the first beast before him, and causeth the earth and them which dwell therein to worship the first beast, whose deadly wound was healed. And he doeth great wonders, so that he maketh fire come down from heaven on the earth in the sight of men, And deceiveth them that dwell on the earth by the means of those miracles which he had power to do in the sight of the beast; saying to them that dwell on the earth, that they should make an image to the beast, which had the wound by a sword, and did live. And he had power to give life unto the image of the beast, that the image of the beast should both speak, and cause that as many as would not worship the image of the beast should be killed.

Verse-by-verse, Dixon found correspondence between John's prophecies and the content of her visions. She saw these passages from Chapter 13 as pointing directly to the "False Prophet" whose mission had been prepared by the "government within a government":

> The social and religious chaos generated by this political machine throughout the United States will prepare the nation for the coming of the prophet of the Antichrist. This political unit of the East will be the tool of the serpent in delivering the masses to him. . . . With teaching and propaganda the prophet will cause people not merely to accept the Antichrist but rather to desire him with positive enthusiasm to create the conditions of his coming and to participate in organizing the frightful and terrifying despotism of his World Empire.

Dixon's scenario was nuanced rather than literalistic, saying that the miracles, signs, and wonders that *Revelations* attributed to the Antichrist and his prophet would not be supernatural events but "the prodigies of science and human achievements." She pointed particularly to the "fire from heaven" spoken of by John, which she saw as the ultimate symbol of the conquest of Nature. "The ideological and falsely scientific prophet" would advance an anti-Christian science perfectly tailored to modern materialism. Finally, she anticipated a full victorious reign of the Antichrist and his prophet, who would be "*specific and identifiable persons!*"

Dixon's celebrity had always been based on the fact that the "specific and identifiable persons" in her visions were almost always noteworthy national and international figures, usually from the world of politics. She gained her initial fame for having successfully predicted the assassinations of Mahatma Gandhi, John and Robert Kennedy, and Martin Luther King, Jr.; the death of Secretary of State John Foster Dulles. Even in her own lifetime, however, Dixon was as widely known for her many wildly inaccurate statements about the future. She predicted: the outbreak of World War III in 1958, in China; that labor leader Walter Reuther would run for President in 1964; that the Russians would land the first man on the moon; that a comet would strike the earth; and that religious warfare would break out all over the world in 1999. It became a national journalistic sport to tally up Jeane Dixon's predictions at year's end; always, the misses outnumbered the hits. A Temple University mathematician coined the phrase "the Jeane Dixon effect," to describe the tendency of a gullible media and public to proclaim a few accurate predictions while overlooking the much larger number of incorrect forecasts.

Believing her faculty of prophecy to have been given by God, Dixon attributed any errors to her own mistakes in interpretation. Indeed, her conservative politics always colored her public predictions, and these can be seen to have been the most erroneous. Calling her perceptions "revelations from God," she claimed to hear the voices of Christ and angels, but she never claimed to be able to call up her gift of prophecy at will. The "Jeane Dixon effect," however true it may be, does not explain the many documented cases in which Dixon described important future events in uncanny detail. Though she made considerable effort to discern it, the most important detail—the actual timing of the Antichrist's appearance—

eluded Jeane Dixon. Believing that she had witnessed his birth in 1962, she thought that the Antichrist would appear in 1992, as a Satanic echo of the fact that Christ's ministry began in his 30th year.

In 1919, Rudolf Steiner had told a small group of listeners: "Before even a small part of the third millennium has run its course, there will be an actual incarnation of Ahriman in the West." Taken together with Jeane Dixon's extraordinary spiritual witnessing of February 5, 1962, Steiner's prediction seems affirmed, and yet the precise timing is still a mystery. The unveiling of this mystery has clearly fallen to Robert Powell, who discovered the timing of the events in Christ's ministry, and thus discovered the "Apocalypse Code." In recent years, Powell has focused much of his scholarly attention on the Galactic Center, and has written a series of books that seem to confirm—along with developments in astronomy and astrophysics—his assertion that humanity is presently moving out of the 500-year-old Copernican worldview to a "Galactic" one.

Much attention has recently focused on the Galactic Center due to popular theories about social and spiritual changes that are expected to occur at the Mayan calendar's "end date" of December 21, 2012. Writers like José Arguelles and Daniel Pinchbeck, seeking to storm the gates of Heaven as surely as Timothy Leary did three generations ago, see the ancient calendar as proof positive of their expectation for a radical expansion of human consciousness, one that will end the greed, the violence, and the materialism that has characterized twentieth century Western history. In astronomical terms, this "Galactic alignment" will see the alignment of the winter solstice sun with the Galactic Equator, due to a movement called the precession of the equinoxes. Along with its daily rotational move-ment and yearly revolution around the sun, the Earth has a much slower movement—a wobble (the astronomers call it "nutation")—that causes the position of the equinoxes and solstices (and all other dates / positions in between) to shift one degree every 71.5 years. Since the sun is a half-degree wide, it takes the December solstice sun half that period—36 years—to precess through the band of the Galactic Equator. Rather than a single moment in time, the "Galac-tic alignment" lasts for a full 36 years, from 1980 to 2016. Robert Powell points out that in the middle of this "Galactic Window" lies the year 1998, a signature year for the Beast, Sorath, whose number *Revelations* gives as 666.

Revelations gives another crucial number for making sense of the significance of the year 2012. Chapter 13 says that the Antichrist shall reign for "two and forty months." If you count backward forty-two *solar* months from December 21, 2012, you come to June 22, 2009, one day after the summer solstice. Counting backward forty-two *synodic* months (the average period of the Moon's revolution with respect to the sun—a sidereal month lasts 27.322 days, while a synodic month lasts 29.531 days) from December 21, 2012, you come to July 31, 2009. Robert Powell points out that *the July 22nd eclipse lies between these two dates, and so reasonably could be said to be "two and forty months" from the 2012 Mayan calendar end date.* 42 months is of course 3½ years, the period of Christ's ministry, which lasted from the Baptism in the Jordan to the Resurrection on Golgotha. Able only to "ape" the Sun Spirit Christ, the Antichrist is fated to "rule" on Earth for this exact same period. On July 22, 2009, Pluto will be at 6° Sagittarius, just 2° from its location at the last temptation of Christ, which signified the opening of the gates of hell. Most provocatively of all, the July 22, 2009 position of Pluto will be just ½° away from where it was at the baptism in the Jordan on September 23, AD 29 (6°53" Sagittarius). July 22, 2009 is the counter-image of the baptism, the eclipse presenting the possibility that Ahriman will descend into a human being, just as Christ entered into Jesus of Nazareth. Ahriman's three and a half year "ministry" then begins...

Only if we allow it to! *Ahriman cannot work without the support of human beings—not just the individual human being who will provide the vehicle for his incarnation, but each and every one of us who remains asleep to the working of Ahriman/Antichrist in the world.* America has a special destiny, an altogether different destiny than that envisioned by the statesmen who held forth in Burlington and Manhattan a hundred years ago. Foreshadowed by the perennially upwelling black, blood sacrificial mysteries in the Valley of Mexico, the continent of America once again is undergoing a confrontation with the forces of evil. Two thousand years ago, a mysterious initiate called Huitzilopochtli bound the black magic of Lucifer and Ahriman by overcoming these adversaries mainly on the *inner planes,* before physically binding the dark Quetzalcoatl-inspired lord upon a cross. We must also do battle on the inner planes, and call forth our inner Sun forces to overcome the eclipse that threatens our consciousness every day. Surrounded by both the web of lies spun by the black magicians of political propaganda and the web of virtual reality spun by digital technology, we are—whether we are conscious of it or not—players in a cosmic drama, a "star war."

"Our" star—the Sun—is a physical expression of the Son of God, who, in our time, has become the "Son of Man," the Etheric Christ being who will receive gratefully the *inner* consecration of our heart forces. The hundredth anniversary of the Etheric Christ's advent—proclaimed in 1909 by Rudolf Steiner –is the real event of 2009! The coming of Ahriman is the shadow event, permitted by world destiny to happen at this time *for our spiritual evolution.*

If July 22, 2009 truly marks the beginning of the Antichrist's 3½-year rulership, and he is preceded by the "false prophet", it seems almost certain that he will come on the world stage very soon, if he is not already present. Along with *Revelations*, two other books of the Bible—the *Second Epistle to the Thessalonians* and the *Book of Daniel*—describe the false prophet as speaking pompous words. *Revelations* and *II Thessalonians* attribute to him "miraculous signs" and say that he will deceive the people and lead them into idolatry. The *Book of Daniel* agrees with *Revelations* about the 3½-year period, suggesting that the false prophet will be destroyed at the return of Jesus Christ. All three books suggest a person of great political power and religious influence, and all point to a person and events of global significance.

The clue as to the identity of the false prophet of the Antichrist lies in another book of the Bible—the *Gospel of Luke*. There is described how, at the Annunciation, the Archangel Gabriel appeared to the Virgin Mary and told her that "the Holy Ghost shall come upon thee," to conceive the Son of God. Gabriel also informed Mary that her cousin Elizabeth, formerly childless, was already six months pregnant. Mary visited Elizabeth in Judea, and when Elizabeth heard Mary's voice, her baby leapt in her womb; this is often seen as John's first act of prophecy. Following the principle that Satan is the "ape of God", it is possible that the false prophet was born six months before the Antichrist, that is, on or about August 5, 1961.

America has a long tradition of mistaking as good that which is very evil. Even as it seems that at this moment we are as a nation wiser, less gullible, more capable of choosing a leader, we must be cautious in light of our long history of following false prophets. The individuals who most readily come to mind—Cotton Mather, Jonathan Edwards, William Miller, Joseph Smith—were religious reformers, but the twentieth century saw the prophetic mantle transferred to more secular figures—William Dudley Pelley, founder of the fascist Silver Legion; anti-Communist crusader Joseph McCarthy; economist Leo Strauss, who birthed the Neoconservatives. Apart from any individual messiahs, America has been continually possessed by a collective messianism, whether the Puritan conception of its colonial experiment as a shining "City on a Hill," the 19th-century belief in manifest destiny, or a more recent rhetorical stance as the bringer of democracy and world-protector against the "Axis of Evil". Our national self-delusion has proved remarkably persistent, regardless of the political party in power. The most enthusiastic singers of national destiny at the 1909 celebrations—Senator Elihu Root, President William Howard Taft— were men whose careers were intertwined with America's rising tide of ruthless, rapacious imperialism. During George W. Bush's presidency, the more damning his rhetoric against perceived enemies abroad, the more likely it was that one could hear his words as an indictment of America itself.

A century ago, America, focusing its attention on the year 1909 as the anniversary of two "discoveries" and their discoverers, engaged in a spectacular episode of both historical commemoration and prophetic envisioning. Flying like Icarus toward the Sun (or Wilbur Wright toward the Statue of Liberty!), America saw nothing but brightness, even though the true Sun—the risen Christ, returning in the etheric realm—went wholly unnoticed. In 2009, much of America stands expectant once again, not because of the 400th anniversary commemorations, but because of the promise that a more cosmic commemoration—the Galactic Alignment—might bring some redemption from the errant ways of the twentieth century.

The crucial date however, is not 2012 but 2009, beginning with the total solar eclipse on July 22nd.

Americans are not particularly good at thinking *mythically* about the plane of history when it is very close to them. It is easy from a century's hindsight to see the limitations of the myths that the Champlain and Hudson tercentenaries were seeking to foster. But to pick up the *New York Times* or the *Burlington Free Press* or any other daily paper and read the headlines through the lens of meta-history, along the lines that Rudolf Steiner laid out a century ago, is much more difficult. The world is too much with us. And yet the times demand that we practice an imaginative, spirit- and soul-filled, while still wholly empirical, investigation into our present, past, and future.

Not a single American newspaper, the day after the attacks on September 11, noticed the terrible threefold completeness of those attacks: the Twin Towers—the lightning calculating, microchip-laden *head* of America; the Pentagon—the nuclear-fisted *arm* of America; and though it escaped injury, the Capitol—the lawmaking *heart* of America. Human thinking, willing, and feeling were all attacked on that day, as the Beast announced his presence in the world, just three years after his number reappeared. The ensuing so-called "War on Terror" is but another sign that the Beast is already afoot in the world.

Today's apocalyptic skywatchers—be they pessimistic Christian evangelicals or romantic seekers of harmonic convergence—simply lack the tools to ply the prophetic trade. Prophecy is a gift of the spiritual world, reserved for a very few individuals whose karma—in the sense of their own freely willed conscious deeds—has led them to be of service to humanity. The world has seen few, if any, prophets on the order of Rudolf Steiner. Humanity does not need, and in fact, cannot abide, more than a handful each century, for enacting destiny takes time, lots of time, and a century for human beings seems to be too short a time to greatly change their ways, even while the cities they build all too rapidly change their contours and customs.

Today, on the spot where the city of Burlington built the grandstand for the Indian pageants, there is a nifty Community Boathouse, offering anyone a chance to get in a sailboat or sea kayak and skim across the dappled surface of Lake Champlain. Nearby, the brick hulk of the old Moran electric generating station makes for a paradoxical ruin, its technology obsolete, but still very much with us.

When the Hudson-Fulton Commission's Naval Parade Committee planned the "Water Gate" at 110th Street and Riverside Park, for the official reception of the *Half Moon* and *Clermont*, they chose a Greek motif, aiming for a sense of permanence, no doubt. Two ninety-foot-high alabaster white Doric columns rose up from the water, so that, for the yachtsmen and sailors and the crews of the *Half Moon* and *Clermont*, plying the waters of *Mahicanituk* in September 1909, the Water Gate was almost as conspicuous as Grant's Tomb, a dozen blocks to the north. "The Water Gate," reads the *Final Report* of the Commission, "effectively demonstrated the desirability of a permanent ceremonial portal at the water of this maritime metropolis." Today, the spot bears the southbound lane of the Henry Hudson Parkway.

Driving past the spot where the Water Gate stood, you used to be able to clearly see the Twin Towers rising from the southern end of the Great Island of the Lenape. From anywhere on the island, they were a gargantuan landmark, an apotheosis of the kind of technological and mercantile greatness that the 1909 celebrants rightly imagined would grace their city a century hence. Their *absence* now would be seen by none of the Hudson-Fulton Commissioners, as it surely is not by the rest of us Americans, as a symbol of our national destiny. And yet, in some future historical reckoning, occasioned or not by a centennial-inspired celebration, perhaps this fabled island will take its proper place in a new story. Each one of us can and must choose how this "short story" will play out; Samuel Champlain, Henry Hudson, and those who followed four hundred years ago faithfully played their parts. Let us now play ours.

A PRAYER,
AND AN INVITATION

IN 1909, a number of prayers were composed and recited as part of the anniversary celebrations. These were prayers of both thanksgiving and supplication. If you glance back at the epigraphs, Burlington Mayor John Burke's and New York Senator Elihu Root's speeches have an element of this, and they also are characteristically materialist in emphasis. As 2009 approaches, I wonder if there will be an impulse toward prayer, and if so, what will be the nature of those prayers. To take hold in the world, prayer needs *silence*, and our 21st century world affords very little silence, especially when large groups of people gather in celebration. America these days is seized by a mania for "festivals"—hyperactive, intense mass gatherings that satiate the senses while leaving the heart hungry. I suspect that the most heartfelt prayers, the ones that will invite the spiritual world to come close, will be those that spring from individual hearts toward the community, as lovers of the Champlain and Hudson Valleys found cooperative ventures like compost projects and community gardens and coop housing; create new community art; build neighborhood relationships; find new and old forms to enrich the lives of their children. These are the initiatives that will keep these regions vibrant and vital.

Living near Lake Champlain, I have the great good fortune to be able to make a daily pilgrimage to various spots along the shoreline, to swim and say my morning prayers. So often I find that others have left silent prayers in the form of whimsical stick and stone and sand sculptures, mute but expressive gestures of celebration of and for the Earth. Built lovingly, reverently, each of these ephemeral creations *is a prayer*, speaking the language of the Angels, and the elemental beings of Nature.

At Easter 1941, during another time of great spiritual trial, the

Russian Christian mystic, scholar and hermetic magician Valentin Tomberg gave this "Meditation on the Etheric Christ." It is even more powerful when accompanied by eurythmy gestures (as taught by Robert Powell):

> Christ is already here.
> From the south of the Earth
> Waves are proceeding from Him across the world.
> Every human being is now able to create a connection
>   with Him
> The human being has to do this out of free will.
> He is opening the path
> to Shamballa,
> And human beings are able to approach Him,
> to create a connection with Him.
> For this, two things are necessary:
> knowledge of Christ
> and Antichrist;
> and aligning oneself
> with Christ.
> If one chooses one of the two streams
> which are now streaming through the world:
> Christ
> or Antichrist
> a radiant blue stream,
> and an ahrimanic stream —
> when one chooses one is already taken
> into one of the two streams.
> Through the Power of Christ one is immeasurably
>   strengthened.
> With Him one can pass through all trials and remain
>   peaceful.
> Through His Power one can endure to an extraordinary
>   degree.
> He bestows great Power.

AUM

I will be carrying this meditation with me in May of 2009, when, as my way of commemorating the 400th anniversaries of Hudson's and Champlain's deeds, I make a pilgrimage from Montreal (where Samuel de Champlain established the short-lived *La Place Royale* colony in 1611) to Manhattan (where I was born, about two miles south of Spuyten Duyvil). By joyfully, mindfully walking the length of these two valleys, I hope to knit them together in my heart, and also knit together the residents of these regions who have in their heart a desire for new stories, new maps, new dreams. Instead of astrolabe and arquebus, I will be packing copies of this book, and a map I've made called "A Corridor of Amity." If you would like to meet and share stories and song and dance along the way, please contact me through my website, "Maps of Wonder":

www.mapsofwonder.com

We'll meet on some shingled Lake Champlain or Hudson River shore, or in a meadow of ripening timothy overlooking these historic waters, or perhaps at one of the many monuments mentioned in this book, and swap stories. You can tell me what you love most about your corner of your valley, and perhaps show me that Tercentenary commemorative medal your grandfather gave you, and I'll teach you the eurythmy movements to accompany the meditation above. And when the smoke blows off from the 400th anniversary fireworks, we can know that there is a community running from the northern headwaters of Lake Champlain to the mouth of the Hudson that is telling and making new stories of American destiny. I look forward to meeting you.

BIBLIOGRAPHICAL ESSAY

I

THOSE WHO WITNESSED the pageantry attending the 1992 Quincentenary celebration of Columbus' landfall may find it difficult to believe that during an earlier era, pageants could influence the historical imagination of an entire generation. On the other hand, we may not find it so difficult to believe that after the generation who witness such spectacles is gone, the elaborate pageants and their many topical messages are soon forgotten. Though the Champlain Tercentenary and the Hudson-Fulton Celebration were the mega-events of their day, comparable to Lee Iacocca's Statue of Liberty extravaganza, they have rarely attracted attention from historians. One exception is David Glassberg's excellent *American Historical Pageantry: The Uses of Tradition in the Early Twentieth Century* (Chapel Hill: University of North Carolina Press, 1990).

It is impossible for me to resist noting that Post Mills, Vermont, was the site of perhaps the most crucial event in the history of the pageantry movement in the United States. The "father" of American historical pageantry, William Chauncy Langdon (whose father, curiously enough, was born in Burlington, and later was deeply involved in YMCA work. Another fact that shows what a small world the past is; Langdon's cousin was New York mayor Seth Low, who was one of the Tercentenary orators) came to Thetford in 1910 to stage a pageant. He had been asked by Charlotte Farnsworth, who ran girls camps in Fairlee. They got $2,500 from the Russell Sage Foundation, (one of the sources later approached by George Henry Perkins's son and fellow UVM professor Henry Perkins for his eugenics work), to see if the pageant might serve as "an agent in social advancement." The motivation was essentially the same as that for the eugenics and Country Life crusades—the fear of "degeneration"—rural depopulation, etc. These fears were rarely voiced by the native hill folk, but were widely shared by the summer people. According to Langdon: "A historical pageant, properly conceived and executed, *could produce an ecstatic communion*, galvanizing Thetford residents in the crusade for the "New Country Life." [italics mine]. The success of the Thetford pageant was a turning point; Langdon became a peripatetic producer of pageants, traveling all over America to stage these events.

Pageants were as important in the pre-cinema era in America in their influence on the popular image of Indians as films have been and continue to be in the twentieth century. Almost all of the historical pageants staged during pageantry's golden era had major scenes featuring Indian groups and characters. There was usually only a cursory attempt to accurately depict Indians. In the case of the Thetford pageant, Langdon visited Thetford three times—to get the job in 1910; to persuade the Thetford Grange to invite outside agricultural experts to town to help in the "revitalization"; and then from June to August of 1911 to rehearse and direct the pageant. Langdon's motto was "the place is the hero," and yet the author of the pageant hardly had ever been to the place. For his Indian material, he wrote to the Smithsonian and to the American Museum of Natural History for information on the Indians of the region.

A curious coincidence worth further exploration for any readers keen on post-Plains Wars "demobilization": on July 27, 1909, a few weeks after the Tercentenary excitement, the Tenth Cavalry—the "Buffalo Soldiers" who had seen action putting down natives in Cuba and the Philippines after their earlier campaigns against the Comanche, Kiowa, Cheyenne, and Arapahoes—arrived at Fort Ethan Allen across the river in Winooski.

For those who would like to read the full text of the Champlain Tercentenary orations, see photos of Tiotiake and the canoe regattas or William Howard Taft in all his corpulent splendor, and relive the whole event, the principal source is Henry W. Hill, editor, *The Champlain Tercentenary: First Report of the New York Lake Champlain Tercentenary Commission*, (Albany: J. B. Lyon Co., 1909; 2nd ed. 1913). Vermont produced a much less ambitious report, *The Tercentenary Celebration of the Discovery of Lake Champlain*, (Montpelier, VT: Capital City Press, 1910). The text of the pageant can be found in the first volume, and in L. O. Armstrong, *The Book of the Play of Hiawatha the Mohawk*, (s. l., s. n., 1909). There is an old note to myself in one of my files that says that the papers of Walter H. Crockett at Special Collections, Bailey-Howe Library, University of Vermont, have lots of Tercentenary material, which I have for some inexplicable reason never managed to peruse. *The Burlington Free Press* served as an interesting window on the events of Tercentenary week, as would the other daily newspapers of the region, especially from those cities that hosted Tercentenary events. Frank Woods' "Spectator" column containing his comments about the Indian pageants are from *The Outlook* 31 July 1909: 784–786. The August 1909 issue of *The Vermonter* is also rich with observations of the festivities.

Though he had been dead for over a decade by 1909, I have the feeling that Francis Parkman was very much a presence at both the Champlain and Hudson celebrations, given how influential his histories had been on the generation of men that planned these events. His comments about Champlain come from *Pioneers of France in the New World* (Little, Brown, and Co., 1907 (1865)) Champlain's remarks are drawn from *The Works of Samuel de Champlain*, general editor H. P. Biggar, Publications of the Champlain Society, 6 volumes (1922–1936), reprinted facsimile, (Toronto: University Press of Toronto, 1971), II: 71. For all of my spleening about what we *won't* learn about the past from the 400th anniversary, the Champlain Quadricentennials (especially Quebec City's 2008 celebration) are inspiring some wonderful new scholarly works. See particularly *Champlain: The Birth of French America*, edited by Raymonde Litalien and Denis Vaugeois; translated by Käthe Roth, (Montréal: McGill-Queen's University Press, 2004). Part VII, "Remembering Champlain" goes more deeply into a number of themes that I only touch upon here.

New York State published an even more lavish report for the Hudson-Fulton Celebration: *The Hudson-Fulton Celebration, 1909, The Fourth Annual Report of the Hudson-Fulton Celebration Commission to the Legislature of the State of New York*, 2 volumes, Edward Hagaman Hall, editor, (Albany: J. B. Lyon Co., 1910). By all means, if your library happens to have a copy of this report, go spend some time browsing the photographs, which quickly transport you into the event's sights and sounds.

When I first got interested in these two events, about twenty years ago, it was before the age of digital search engines, and though I admit that I miss the romance (and musty smell!) of leafing through back issues of the *Burlington Free Press*, I do not miss the hassle of doing microfilm research in the *New York Times*. Thank you, thank you, thank you, Mr. Arthur Ochs Sulzberger, Jr., and anyone else at the *Times* who is responsible for the (free!) online archive of this wonderful newspaper.

Henry Adams' experience at the Paris Exposition of 1900 makes up Chapter 25 in *The Education of Henry Adams* (Boston: Houghton Mifflin, 1961).

II

When I first encountered the writings of Rudolf Steiner some 17 years ago, while doing doctoral dissertation research on the history of scientific and artistic interest in synaesthesia, I was dumbfounded, slack-jawed, and absolutely smitten. A handful of art historians attributed to Steiner a profound influence on Wassily Kandinsky's pioneering efforts to produce abstract art. The seemingly routine research task of double-checking these scholars' assertions led me on an intellectual and spiritual journey for which I shall always be grateful. These scholars were, by the way, quite wrong; you can read the real story about Steiner and Kandinsky in my *Bright Colors Falsely Seen: Synaesthesia and the Search for Transcendental Knowledge* (Yale University Press: 1998).

Within the academic world, wildly incorrect, secondhand, and often outright hostile assertions are the norm when it comes to Rudolf Steiner; the reliable scholarship and interpretation of Steiner's profound spiritual gift to humanity lies almost entirely within anthroposophical publishing circles. I began my own journey into Steiner's works with the wonderful book, *The Essential Steiner*, edited and introduced by Robert MacDermott (Hudson, NY: Lindisfarne Books, 2007). SteinerBooks editor Christopher Bamford's brilliant introductory essays to dozens of Steiner lecture cycles make for rich and rewarding exploration in their own right, and serve as a helpful friend as one enters the challenging realm of Steiner's thought and deeds. Thankfully, there are an increasing number of authors who have joined Bamford and McDermott as guides; the most magisterial work of "introduction" is the three-volume "Bible and Anthroposophy" series of Edward Reaugh Smith: *The Burning Bush: Rudolf Steiner, Anthroposophy and the Holy Scriptures: Terms & Phrases* (1997); *David's Question: What Is Man? (Psalms* 8:4) (2001); and *The Soul's Long Journey: How the Bible Reveals Reincarnation* (2003).

Given the breadth and depth of Rudolf Steiner's intellectual legacy, and the scope of his accomplishments, the narrow window that I have opened upon him in this book may seem unfair, if not downright misguided. My intention here has been to approach Steiner as a historical actor, one of immensely greater significance than the other actors who appear in the signal year of 1909, but one who can be known quite intimately through his words alone. Having attempted but largely failed elsewhere (*Across the Great Border Fault: The Naturalist Myth in America* (Rutgers University Press: 2000) to present Steiner within a twentieth century American cultural historical context, limiting him here largely to the year 1909 will I hope make him more accessible.

With this much said, it still seems wholly unfair to point the uninitiated reader to the "raw" lectures of Rudolf Steiner; but here are my sources for this chapter. The 1909 Cassel cycle is published as Rudolf Steiner, *The Gospel of St. John and Its Relation to the Other Gospels*, (Hudson, NY: SteinerBooks, 1982). For this and many other Steiner lecture cycles, my Cajun friend Bobby Matherne has written an excellent "review" which will open rewarding avenues of exploration; see his "A Reader's Journal" site at: *http://www.doy letics.com/arj*. For the January 25, 1910 lecture on the advent of the Etheric Christ, and the subsequent lectures that explain this further, see *The Reappearance of Christ in the Etheric*, (SteinerBooks, 2003). For the Dusseldorf cycle, a wonderful new edition has just been published: *The Spiritual Hierarchies and the Physical World: Zodiac, Planets & Cosmos* (SteinerBooks, 2008). Thanks to James Stewart, creator of the online Rudolf Steiner Archive, an enormous number of lectures (and books) can be read online at: *http://www.rsarch ive.org/index.php*. The site is very easy to use, and includes both chronological listings of onsite lectures and full chronological lists of all of Steiner's lectures, year-by-year. Thank you James!

The discovery of the Jupiter-rhythm as the rhythm for Christ's descent through the hierarchies was made by Robert Powell; see his articles in the journal *Shoreline:* "Reflections on the Second Coming" (*Shoreline* 2, 1989) and "Sub-Nature and the Second Coming" (*Shoreline* 3, 1990), which have been republished in his book *The Christ Mystery: Reflections on the Second Coming* (Fair Oaks, CA: Rudolf Steiner College Press, 1999). There is also an extended discussion of this in "The Second Coming and the New Age," Chapter 9 of Powell's *Hermetic Astrology: Volume II* (San Rafael, CA: Sophia Foundation Press, 2007—first published in 1989). On the 1 year:100 year correspondence between the life of an individual and the life of humanity, see Appendix II in *Hermetic Astrology: Volume I* (1987). For an explanation of how Rudolf Steiner was able to experience Christ's etheric return in advance of 1933, see Robert Powell, *Chronicle of the Living Christ: The Life and Ministry of Jesus Christ: Foundations of Cosmic Christianity*, (Hudson, NY: SteinerBooks, 1996).

Citing these works of Robert Powell in such a dispassionate manner seems odd, for he is my close friend and colleague. This book owes its greatest debt to the understandings Robert has imparted to me over the last seven years. My encounter in the year 1999 with the last mentioned work—*Chronicle of the Living Christ*—was a life-changing event; the exposition of the timing of Christ's reappearance in the etheric realm and its historical effects in the Afterword to *Chronicle of the Living Christ* planted the seed for this book.

Though notes have been preserved from Steiner's January 6, 1909 lecture in Munich on the karmic relationships of Novalis, Raphael, John the Baptist, and the prophet Elijah, its significance is explored thoroughly in Sergei Prokofieff's *Eternal Individuality: Toward a Karmic Biography of Novalis*, (London: Temple Lodge, 1992). Prokofieff explores the mystery of the "two Johns" in a much abbreviated work, *The Mystery of John the Baptist and John the Evangelist at the Turning Point of Time: An Esoteric Study*, (Temple Lodge, 2005). Another very helpful recent work is Charles S. Tidball, with Robert Powell, *Jesus, Lazarus, and the Messiah: Unveiling Three Christian Mysteries*, (Hudson, NY: SteinerBooks, 2005).

Steiner revealed in 1909 an even greater mystery—the mystery of the two Jesus children—which I have totally passed over in this chapter. For the lectures that introduce this to the world, see Rudolf Steiner, *According to Luke: The Gospel of Compassion and Love Revealed*, (SteinerBooks, 2001). A very helpful companion to penetrating this awesome aspect of the Christian story is Edward Reaugh Smith's *The Incredible Births of Jesus*, (SteinerBooks, 1998).

As long as I am speaking of mysteries, the other one that I gloss over in Chapter Two is that of the Christ rhythm in history, first revealed to humanity by Rudolf Steiner in his lecture "Et Incarnatus Est: The Time Cycle in Historical Events" on December 23, 1917. This is again an example of Steiner's loving circumspection applied to his spiritual research, for he gave only the most elementary indications during his lifetime about this rhythm. Of Steiner's students who have elucidated the 33⅓-year-rhythm further, three of the best works are: Robert Powell, *Chronicle of the Living Christ* (see the Afterword); Peter Tradowsky, *Kaspar Hauser: The Struggle for the Spirit* (Temple Lodge, 1998), and Terry Boardman, *Kaspar Hauser: Where Did He Come From?* (Wynstones Press, 2006). I speak briefly of the Christ rhythm in Henry Thoreau's life in *Expect Great Things: The Life of Henry David Thoreau* (forthcoming).

Henry Adams' essay, "The Rule of Phase Applied to History," was published posthumously in *The Degradation of the Democratic Dogma* (New York: Kessinger, 1919). For thermodynamics and history of science geeks, you can triangulate this fascinating episode in Adams career by way of Keith R. Burich's "Henry Adams, the Second Law of Thermodynamics, and the Course of History," *Journal of the History of Ideas*, 48(3) (1987): pp 467–482.

III

Poor Charles Fort would undoubtedly turn over in his grave if he could see what sort of epistemological shenanigans are now performed in his name. Anyone who has encountered Fort by way of *Fortean Times* or *The Anomalist* magazines would do well to run, not walk, to their nearest library and read any single chapter in one of these works by Fort: *The Book of the Damned*, (Prometheus

Books, 1999 (1919)); *New Lands*, (Ace Books, 1941 (1923)); *Lo!*, (Ace Books, 1941 (1931)); *Wild Talents*, (Ace Books, 1932). Dover has done us all a favor by issuing the *Complete Books of Charles Fort*, (New York: Dover Publications, 1998). You can also find the online at Mr. X's website at: *http://www.resologist.net/index.htm.*

In encouraging and shepherding any first time reader of Charles Fort, I could do no better than the anonymous contributor to the Wikipedia entry on Fort: "Understanding Fort's books takes time and effort: his style is complex, violent and poetic, satirical and subtle, profound and occasionally puzzling. Ideas are abandoned and then recalled a few pages on; examples and data are offered, compared and contrasted, conclusions made and broken, as Fort holds up the unorthodox to the scrutiny of the orthodoxy that continually fails to account for them. Pressing on his attacks, Fort shows what he sees as the ridiculousness of the conventional explanations and then interjects with his own theories."

All these caveats, however, miss the fact that FORT IS FUN!!! The Super-Sargasso Sea is just the beginning. I had to practice enormous restraint in this chapter, since the witty one liners and page-long rants are simultaneously devastating critiques of modern materialist thought and side-splittingly funny flights of linguistic fancy. A project that I have dreamed of for years now is to do a combined biographical and literary exploration of Rudolf Steiner and Charles Fort. Lo! That damned book of new lands would take some wild talents.

If you are one of those skeptical inquirers who has wittingly or unwittingly perverted Fort's work, and are looking back here for bibliographical minutiae with which to discredit *this* book, BOO! When you have recovered yourself and wish to follow up on my Fort references, you can begin with the following chapters/works. *Lo!* Part I: chapter 2 describes the British airship flap of 1909; part III: chapter 1 touches on the fires at Messina, 1908. *Book of the Damned* deals with "sulphurous stuff" in chapter 6, before launching into meditations on comets (chapter 10); oddly-inscribed stones (chapter 11); fairy crosses (chapter 12); poltergeists (chapter 13); Thunderbirds against the sun (chapter 16); earthquakes and fireballs (chapter 17); little green men (chapter 18); the 1898 airship flap (chapter 20); ball lightning (chapter 23); things 'meteoric' (chapter 24); the Burlington 1907 explosion (chapter 25); and concludes with a description of cloven-hoofed footprints in the snow in South Devonshire, England in 1889. *New Lands* itemizes a string of "skyquakes" in Chapter 17 and 22, with a very entertaining chapter (18) on sea serpents in between. In part II, chapter 3, Fort examines the co-incidence of earth-quakes, earth-booms, and earth-lights. chapter 7's "Exclusionism" is priceless Thomas Kuhn meets Monty Python. *Wild Talents* is the work I know least, and though I have not drawn on the book for any of this chapter, I am happy to draw your attention toward chapter 7 on incidents of cattle mutilation, chapter 8 on vampires, and the final chapter, where the enigmatic John Worrell Keely of Philadelphia is the subject. Some future metahistorian will have a field day perhaps tracing Keely's karmic roots back to the 7th century Academy of Gondhishapur.

Rudolf Steiner's lecture of January 1, 1909, "Mephistopheles and Earthquakes," was published as lecture 2 in the pamphlet *The Deed of Christ and the Opposing Spiritual Powers*, (London: Rudolf Steiner Publishing Company, 1954).

My impressions of the UVM Kakewalk come mainly from perusing old programs (University Archives at UVM has a fairly complete set), the *Cynic, Burlington Free Press*, and *Ariel* (the UVM yearbook). Jim Loewen's "Black Image in White Vermont" in R. V. Daniels, *The University of Vermont: The First Two Hundred Years* (Hanover, NH: University Press of New England, 1991) provides a good overview of Kakewalk's history, including a fairly detailed look at its demise.

IV

On Champlain's likeness, see Denis Martin, "Discovering the Face of Samuel de Champlain" in *Champlain: The Birth of French America*, (2004).

The brief indications that Rudolf Steiner left regarding both the physical nature and the spiritual effect of comets are another invitation to a rich new research program, and I hope that—given the continued role of comets in our own time—someone may be inspired from the curious juxtaposition I present here to take up the task. R. S. W. Bobbette has made a survey of Steiner's remarks about comets that will serve as an introduction to this undertaking: *Introductory Essays on Rudolf Steiner's Star-Knowledge: The Cosmic Feminine: Steiner's View of Cometary Life* (1998). This can be found online at *http://wn.rsarchive.org/RelArtic/BobbetteRSWsteiner2_008.html*.

The critical June 29, 1908 lecture of Rudolf Steiner on Sorath, given on the eve of the Tunguska explosion, can be found in *The Apocalypse of St. John: Lectures on the Book of Revelation*, (SteinerBooks, 1993). The 1919 lectures discussed in this chapter are collected in *The Influences of Lucifer and Ahriman: Human Responsibility for the Earth*, (SteinerBooks, 1993). See also "The Book of Revelation and the Work of the Priest" (Lecture 16, Dornach 20 Sept. 1924).

Two works are of enormous assistance in understanding Rudolf Steiner's teachings about Sorath: Peter Tradowsky, *Christ and Antichrist: Understanding the Events at the End of the Century and Recognizing Our Tasks*, (London: Temple Lodge, 1998) and Sergei O. Prokofieff, *The Encounter with Evil and Its Overcoming Through Spiritual Science*, (Temple Lodge, 1999). Tradowsky is especially helpful in seeing the workings of Sorath in National Socialism. See also his short work *'Ere the Century Closes: A Contribution to an Understanding of Our Time*, (North Yorkshire, England: Camphill Books, 1995). Ian Kershaw's biography of Hitler is *Hitler 1889–1936 Hubris*, (New York: W.W. Norton, 1998).

Robert Powell links the chronology of Nazification to parallel events in the first century in *Chronicle of the Living Christ*, pp 418–422. Powell demonstrates how the rhythmically recurring "etheric remembrance" of the last three and one-half years of Jesus' life—the period between the baptism in the Jordan and the Crucifixion and Resurrection—is a time of particularly strong benevolent influence of Christ upon humanity, and how during these periods there are renewed attacks to counter this influence. In the twentieth century he points to the periods June 29, 1929 to January 8, 1933; October 27, 1962 to May 9, 1966; and February 24, 1996 to September 6, 1999. In the first period, during which Christ was working to effect an awakening among humanity to the inner power of the etheric body, opposition arose in the false outer power of the Führer. In the second period, when Christ awakened humanity to impulses of brotherhood and community, opposition arose in the form of the drug culture. Powell sees the last period, through which we have just passed, as the time when the most important impulse of the Second Coming should be awakened—the knowledge of the living being of Nature. Powell sees the global environmental movement as a manifestation of this impulse; he finds its opposition in the widespread fascination with virtual reality, the substitution of lifeless images for living reality. Powell interprets these three historical oppositions during the twentieth century as repetitions of Christ's temptations in the desert as described in the Gospel of Matthew: Period 1: "If you will fall down and worship me" (Matt. 4:9) = the temptations of the will to power; Period 2: "Casting oneself down from the pinnacle of the temple" (Matt. 4:5) = the hedonistic surrender to instinctual urges that dim the faculty of reason; Period 3: "Turn[ing] stones into bread" (Matt. 4:3) = the embrace of ersatz life, that is, "stones."

About twenty years ago, I stumbled on Byron Clark's scrapbooks in the attic of the YMCA on College Street in Burlington, while researching the history of Camp Abnaki. A fire destroyed much of Clark's archival material, but somehow his photo albums survived, and they offer a tantalizing glimpse of almost three decades of summers of playing Indian, and a unique portrait of the cult of manliness at the opening of the century.

V

I have been in love with the American Museum of Natural History since my first visit there as a fourth grader in 1968. I dream of reincarnating a century or two hence to become the curator of this great museum, at a time when the Trustees are ready to reorganize it according to Rudolf Steiner's esoteric cosmology, zoology, and anthropology. The publication done by the Museum for the Hudson-Fulton Celebration was "The Indians of Manhattan Island and Vicinity" (Anthropological Papers of the AMNH #3, 1909), authored by an all star cast of New York city area naturalists: Clark Wissler, Alanson Skinner, James K. Finch, Reginald Pelham Bolton, Mark Raymond Harrington, Max Schrabisch, and Frank G. Speck.

As a student of American history, I at times get frustrated by Rudolf Steiner's Eurocentrism; the only two Americans whom he researched in the Akashic record were Ralph Waldo Emerson and Woodrow Wilson, and aside from the occasional comment about the etheric geography of North America, Frederick Winslow Taylor's time-motion studies as a symptom of mechanical occultism, or indictments of the Fox sisters and their Spiritualist descendants, one is hard-pressed to find Steiner as a source of direct insight into America. Still, in his two 1916 lectures on the "Mexican Mysteries" Steiner surely did more than any early twentieth century American historian to illuminate the hidden history of the upstart nation. The lectures are online at the Rudolf Steiner Archive, and in *Inner Impulses of Evolution: The Mexican Mysteries and the Knights Templar*, (Hudson, NY: Anthroposophical Press, 1984). Stephen Clarke, who runs a BMW shop in Albuquerque, New Mexico, has brought his wit and wisdom to bear on these lectures in a series of essays called "American Chapters," which can be found online at *http:// www.eleggua.com/Spirit/Stephen%20Clarke/RSMM-2.htm.*

More historical background on the UVM Museum can be found in my articles: "The College of Natural History at the University of Vermont, 1826–1850," *Vermont History* (1985): 77–94 and "The Natural Sciences and George Henry Perkins" in Robert V. Daniels, editor, *The University of Vermont: The First Two Hundred Years*, (Hanover: University Press of New England, 1991). The second article suggests my principal sources for George Henry Perkins—the Perkins Papers in University Archives at UVM, student notebooks, and Perkins' own publications. Most of the latter have been collected by a descendant and bound together in one volume that is in the University Archives collection of Perkins material. Perkins' original museum catalogue is housed at the Fleming Museum.

The Spanish historical accounts discussed in this chapter are Bernardino Sahagún, *Florentine Codex: History of the Things of New Spain*, translated and edited by Arthur J.O. Anderson and Charles Dibble, (University of Utah Press, 1950–1982) and Diego Durán, *The History of the Indies of New Spain*, Doris Heyden, ed., Civilization of the American Indian series, #210, Norman: University of Oklahoma Press (1994). In the last 30 years, there has been an explosion of scholarship on the Mexica and their antecedent civilizations, and I apologize for not drawing on that scholarship more extensively. For the beginning reader, there is still no better survey of the Mexica world at the time of Spanish contact than Miguel Léon-Portilla's *The Broken Spears: The Aztec Account of the Conquest of Mexico*, (Boston: Beacon Press, 1992 (1962). Léon-Portilla discusses Tlacaellel's role in the Foreword. I would have liked to have been able to say more here about the relationship between Aztec myth and the remarkable sacrificial stone bearing the image of Coyolxauhqui found in 1978 during underground work near the Zocalo in Mexico City. See particularly Eduardo Matos Moctezuma, "Archaeology & Symbolism in Aztec Mexico: The Templo Mayor of Tenochtitlan," *Journal of the American Academy of Religion*, Vol. 53, No. 4 (Dec., 1985), pp 797–813.

On Christ's descent into the underworld, see Robert Powell's "Sub-Nature and the Second Coming" (*Shoreline* 3, 1990 — republished in 1999 in *The Christ Mystery: Reflections on the Second Coming*) and his *The Most Holy Trinosophia: The New Revelations of the Divine Feminine*, (SteinerBooks, 2000). See also Rudolf Steiner, *The Interior of the Earth: An Esoteric Study of the Subterranean Spheres* (Forest Row, England: Rudolf Steiner Press, 2006), Sigismund von Gleich, *The Transformation of Evil and the Subterranean Spheres of the Earth*, (Temple Lodge, 2005) and Chapter 9 in Sergei O. Prokofieff, *The Cycle of the Year as a Path of Initiation Leading to an Experience of the Christ Being: An Esoteric Study of the Festivals*, (Temple Lodge, 1995).

I hope to take up Cyrus Pringle's story more fully in a companion volume to this work; you can read more about him in my *Lewis Creek Lost and Found* (University Press of New England: 2001).

Regarding the reading of the symbols on Juan Diego's tilma, see the "Our Lady of Guadalupe," article at: *http://www.bridegroom press.com/snippets/guadhandout.pdf.*

VI

Joseph Clarke's Hudson-Fulton ode is published in Volume II of the official report. America's affinity for historical commemoration at the opening of the twentieth century was accompanied by an outpouring of poetry on historical themes. A *New York Times* editorial (September 29, 1909) lamented the flood of mediocre poetry inspired by the 1909 commemoration: "Our advice to everybody who feels an uncontrollable impulse to sing the Hudson River is to go ahead and do it, but do not assume that because the impulse was uncontrollable the voice was loud and clear enough to deserve a public hearing."

It is not completely fair of me to say that women were excluded from the Hudson-Fulton celebration's official banquet. The *Hudson-Fulton Report* gives the full story: "Although the sentiment of the Commission was in favor of admitting ladies to the tables, the physical limitations of the banquet hall compelled the Committee to restrict the tickets to gentlemen only. So far as the boxes in the gallery permitted, however, the banquet was graced by the presence of the ladies."

For images of the Malsch building and the Goetheanum, and a description of the process by which these arose, see *Rosicrucianism Renewed: The Unity of Art, Science & Religion* (SteinerBooks, 2007) and Van James, *Spirit and Art: Pictures of the Transformation of Consciousness*, (SteinerBooks, 2001).

Steiner's April 29, 1909 lecture is published as *Isis and Madonna*, (Mercury Press, 1987). The lecture where he speaks of Christ acting in concert with the entire cosmos was given on June 8, 1911; it can be found in *The Spiritual Guidance of the Individual and Humanity: Some Results of Spiritual-Scientific Research into Human History and Development*, (Anthroposophic Press, 1991). Sergei Prokofieff, in *The Spiritual Origins of Eastern Europe and the Future Mysteries of the Holy Grail*, (Temple Lodge, 1993) (see note 140, pp 513–514), gives the most complete explanation for the Goetheanum fire.

Rudolf Steiner's remark about the 1 year = 100 years relationship of Sophia to humanity is in a lecture he gave on January 30, 1923; see *Awakening to Community*, (SteinerBooks, 1974). The quote from Rudolf Steiner about the twentieth century confrontation with evil is from lecture 4 (October 25, 1918) in the cycle *From Symptom to Reality in Modern History*, (London: Rudolf Steiner Books, 1976).

The remarks about Pluto and Hamal in Steiner's natal chart are from Robert Powell's introduction (pp 10–11) to the *Christian Star*

Calendar 2005. Following Robert Powell's indications about mega-stars, much more might be said about a number of the events mentioned in this book. See Powell, *General Introduction to the Christian Star Calendar: A Key to Understanding*, (Eugene, Oregon: Sophia Foundation of North America, 2003) and Powell and Dann, *The Astrological Revolution: Unveiling the Science of the Stars As a Science of Reincarnation and Karma* (forthcoming). In addition, each issue of the *Christian Star Calendar* (San Rafael, CA: Sophia Foundation Press) since the 2004 edition includes the megastars as part of the calendar annotations.

In his *Hermetic Astrology I* (pp 220, 451) and *Hermetic Astrology II* (pp121, p409), Robert Powell gives Rudolf Steiner's full horoscope and birth data. Robert Powell, "Pluto and the Galactic Center," *Christian Star Calendar* 2007, (San Rafael: Sophia Foundation Press, 2007). The sidereal locations of Pluto, Sun and Moon for the different events mentioned comes from Robert Powell, *Christian Hermetic Astrology: The Star of the Magi and the Life of Christ*, (Anthroposophic Press, 1998), pp 48–49, and *Hermetic Astrology II*, pp 333–338.

In this and subsequent chapters I use the word "sidereal" without explaining it—please forgive me. Literally meaning "pertaining to the stars," the sidereal zodiac differs from the tropical zodiac (the one in use by almost all contemporary Western astrology) in that it ties its signs of the zodiac to the actual constellations, taking account of the precession of the equinoxes (a shift of about one degree every 72 years). From *The Astrological Revolution*:

"The *sidereal zodiac*—not the tropical zodiac of traditional Western astrology—is the authentic astrological zodiac. The sidereal zodiac is the original zodiac of the Babylonian, Egyptian, Greek, and Roman astrologers, and it—or a close variant thereof—is used to the present day in Hindu astrology; in contrast to traditional Western astrology that utilizes the tropical astrology used by Arab astrologers, based on the tropical zodiac that was introduced into the West in the middle of the twelfth century AD, when Arabic astrological texts were translated into Latin. Whereas the sidereal zodiac divides the circle of zodiacal constellations into twelve equal stellar signs, i.e., equal-length constellations each 30 degrees long, the tropical zodiac is defined to commence with the vernal point, where the Sun is located on March 21, and is thus of a calendrical nature, bearing no relationship to the zodiacal constellations."

The shift from the sidereal to the tropical zodiac has been an important aspect of the loss of the ancient star wisdom, and thus, of losing Sophia. Robert Powell's work, *History of the Zodiac*, (San Rafael, California: Sophia Academic Press, 2007) is a landmark work signifying the advent of the recovery of Sophia's star wisdom.

Robert Juet's account of the 1609 voyage was most recently published as *Juet's Journal: The Voyage of the Half Moon From 4 April to 7 November* 1609, edited by Robert M. Lunny (Collections of the New Jersey Historical Society, v. 12. The Hudson River Maritime Museum has an excellent site with links to various editions of Juet's Journal, along with other resources; see *http://www.hrmm.org/halfmoon/halfmoon.htm*.

It took 30 years before a statue of Henry Hudson was finally added to the top of the obelisk on Spuyten Duyvil Hill. In our own era, of course, Spuyten Duyvil is well renowned as the body of water ('Spuyten Devil Cove') next to the estate of the X-Men, some of whose superpowers are a kind of uncanny caricature of Sorath's.

VII

On the St. Mark Group and the history of the New York region's anthroposophical groups, see Henry Barnes, *Into The Heart's Land: A Century Of Rudolf Steiner's Work In North America*, (Steiner-Books, 2005) and also my *Across the Great Border Fault: The Naturalist Myth in America*. *Initiation and Its Results* was the sequel to *The Way of Initiation or How to Attain Knowledge of the Higher Worlds*; the two works were extensively rewritten and appeared in first appeared in 1923 as *Knowledge of the Higher Worlds and Its Attainment*. The book gives instruction on how to consciously obtain first-hand knowledge of spiritual realities.

In the discussion of Robert Powell's work, I have presented a chronology that may give the impression that his work *Chronicle of the Living Christ* (1996) was his first publication to precisely date the events in Jesus Christ's life. This was actually done in his 1991 work, *Christian Hermetic Astrology: The Star of the Magi and the Life of*

Christ, the third volume in a trilogy (including the two-volume *Hermetic Astrology*) dedicated to the new star wisdom. Although the reader may feel that the discussion of zodiacal configurations in this chapter is overly technical, the material actually merits *more* technical elaboration, however, I felt that this would interrupt the narrative. The empirical truth of these new discoveries lies in the technical details, and one of the objectives of this book is to encourage others with the requisite technical skills to undertake the task of corroborating Powell's findings, which indeed are completely revolutionary.

A recent edition of Anne Catherine Emmerich's report of her visions is in four volumes: *The Life of Jesus Christ* (Rockford, IL: Tan Books and Publications, 2004); an earlier edition (1914) is available online at *http://www.jesus-passion.com/DOLOROUS_ PASSION_ OF_OUR_LORD_JESUS_CHRIST.htm*.

Charles Fort's discussion of eclipses is from Chapter 17 of *Book of the Damned*. Rudolf Steiner's lecture on eclipses, on June 25, 1922, is available online at *http://wn.rsarchive.org/Lectures/Places/Dor na ch/19220625p01.html*. Robert Powell's "The Eclipse of March 29, 2006," was published in the Steiner Books 2006 Spring Reader catalog. It is also available online, along with another article by Robert Powell, "After the Eclipse," from the Sophia Foundation of North America: *http://sophiafoundation.org/articles*.

The discussion of Jeane Dixon's February 1962 vision is drawn from Chapters 8 and 9 of *My Life and Prophecies* (NY: William Morrow).

As I mention in the preface, I had for many years had an uncanny sense of something significant about the year 2009, and so, when I encountered Wain Farrants' article, "The Continuing Influence of the Grand Conjunction of 1962: An Imagination for the 21st Century," in the 2006 edition of the *Christian Star Calendar*, I felt my hunch had been confirmed. This sense redoubled with Wain Farrants' follow-up article, "The Reign of the Antichrist, the Unlawful Prince of the World," in the *Christian Star Calendar* 2007. These are profoundly important works of research, and I feel it is critical to point out that they have been undertaken by someone who is not clairvoyant. I say this as encouragement to anyone—like myself—who has only their own inner beacon for the truth to guide them. Indeed, without this, any forms of clairvoyance are useless, if not dangerous.

For the past eight years, I have been a witness to and participant in Robert Powell's extraordinary mission of preparing a path of initiation for the new mysteries of Christ and Sophia. The discussion on the last pages of this book regarding the "2012 Window" and the timing of Ahriman's incarnation come from lectures that Robert has given in just the last few months—between April and July of 2008. In treating these extremely sensitive topics, I have tried to follow his example of practicing equanimity and objectivity, but I fear that my discussion here reduces Robert's pioneering spiritual research to a mere scholarly endeavor. Bringing forward both knowledge of the Antichrist, and the content and the practice (sacred and cosmic dance) for overcoming Antichrist through the true power of Christ, Robert Powell is performing an unparalleled deed for humanity in our time.

The only original contribution that I can claim to have made to the startling suggestions of this last chapter is to have noticed the resonance of Pluto's location at the July 22, 2009 eclipse with the position at 9° Sagittarius on November 29, AD 29, and the linking of the June 28, 1908 eclipse to the Tunguska event.

From a host of New Age authors who deal with the subject of the Mayan calendar 2012 date, I single out José Arguelles and Daniel Pinchbeck, perhaps because I am both most familiar with their writings, and because they have the widest audiences. Daniel Pinchbeck's 2012: *The Return of Quetzalcoatl*, (Los Angeles: Tarcher, 2006), for all of its optimism, is tragically symptomatic of the historical myopia that continues to afflict American Romantics. Daniel's earlier work, *Breaking Open the Head: A Psychedelic Journey into the Heart of Contemporary Shamanism*, (Broadway Books, 2002) contains a lucid, faithful primer on Rudolf Steiner's thought. Some future historian will have a field day tracing the roots and shoots of Arguelles' intellectual and spiritual legacy.

You may be curious as to what is meant by the first chapter's subtitle—"Apogee." For at least twenty years now, I've been haunted by the intuition of some deep connection between the years 1909 and 2009. Now that we've come to the *perigee* of 2009—the closest approach to this signal year—I had the sense of 1909 as *apogee*, at least in the sense of it being the starting place for these investigations, and the year that lies farthest from our present moment. If you've made it this far, congratulations—Samuel de Champlain and Henry Hudson would be proud of your perseverance!